Program Advocacy

PROGRAM ADVOCACY
POWER, PUBLICITY, AND THE TEACHER-LIBRARIAN

Ken Haycock

1990
LIBRARIES UNLIMITED, INC.
Englewood, Colorado

Readings selected from the journal *Emergency Librarian*
published by
Dyad Services
Box C34069, Department 284
Seattle, Washington 98124-1069
and
P.O. Box 46258, Station G
Vancouver, British Columbia V6R 4G6

LIBRARIES UNLIMITED, INC.
P.O. Box 3988
Englewood, CO 80155-3988

Program Advocacy: Power, Publicity, and the Teacher-Librarian is copublished with Dyad Services.

In this book, readers may note some inconsistencies in spelling, usage, and referencing styles. These differences are due to the nature of these readings, taken from previously published articles and written by a variety of authors of different nationalities.

Library of Congress Cataloging-in-Publication Data

Program advocacy : power, publicity, and the teacher-librarian /
  [edited by] Ken Haycock.
    xii, 105 p. 22x28 cm.
    Includes bibliographical references.
    ISBN 0-87287-781-7
    1. School libraries--Administration--Political aspects. 2. School
libraries--Aims and objectives. 3. Public relations--School
libraries. 4. Libraries and community. 5. Libraries and education.
6. Teacher-librarians.   I. Haycock, Ken.
Z675.S3P7527   1990
027.8'223--dc20   89-78042
                                 CIP

Contents

Part 2
THE COMMITMENT

Part 3
THE STRATEGIES

**Part 4
THE CONCLUSION**

*A Special Message
From The Former
Prime Minister of Canada
Pierre Elliott Trudeau*

CANADA

I am happy to extend my greetings to the Editor, staff, and readers of <u>Emergency Librarian</u>.

A trip to the school's library resource centre is a valuable part of a student's curriculum: it allows the student time to learn the necessary skills for finding and retrieving information. The teacher-librarian plays an important role in the development and integration of these skills into instructional programs for group teaching. In our information-rich age, research and study skills will become increasingly important, and will focus more attention on the part of the teacher-librarian, as an integral member of the school staff.

My very best wishes to all school librarians.

Ottawa
1 9 8 2

Part 1
THE PRODUCT

Teacher-librarians need to speak with a strong, unified voice about the value of resource-based teaching and learning and their role in the educational enterprise. We have nothing to apologize for but neither can we presume that the need for support for school resource centers is self-evident and without question.

Bev Anderson provides an overview of the key points coming out of a major research project undertaken by the Calgary (Alberta) Board of Education. School resource centers and teacher-librarians are important and they do make a difference to teaching and learning! This type of evidence is more common than we believe and should be used with school administrators and other decision-makers. Shirley Fitzgibbons likewise provides substantial support for our value and the difference which we make in her review of the research on library services for children and young adults. At *Emergency Librarian* we make every attempt to bring research evidence to the attention of our readers in a way that can be used with educators. The "What Works: Research—The Implications for Professional Practice" columns are modeled on the "What Works" reviews produced by the U.S. Department of Education. Use these to good advantage!

While school librarians are clearly first and foremost professional teachers (hence our use of the term "teacher-librarian"), there are other library associations and groups which have a vested interest in the promotion of all types of libraries and services, yet we rarely call on these natural allies. The British Columbia Library Association (which neither includes teacher-librarians nor represents school resource centers) prepared the brief included here for major public budget sessions. We need to develop these links even more.

When teacher-librarians can visualize their product and clearly project that vision, we will be in a far better position to help others to share our vision and move forward together to make it a reality.

School Libraries – Definitely Worth Their Keep

Bev Anderson

When dollars are devoted to school library services, is there corresponding value for students? An evaluation of school library programs in the Calgary Board of Education suggests that the answer is "Yes!" The evaluation project measured the extent of library service, the skill level and attitudes of students and the resource allocation and background characteristics of 65 sample schools. Findings indicate that when there was sufficient staff time and resource budget, teacher-librarians performed a role of school-based consultant and were able to provide audio-visual services. When this expanded role occurred, there was corresponding increase in student skills, positive student attitudes and assistance for teachers.

BACKGROUND

In 1977, the Chief Superintendent of the Calgary Board of Education commissioned an evaluation of school library/resource centre programs. The purpose of this evaluation was to investigate the question "Is the Board receiving sufficient value for the dollars that are/have been devoted to school resource services?"[1] Specific direction was provided to include qualitative and quantitative data regarding the effects of resource services upon students. Rather than circulation statistics or reading preferences, the evaluation was to assess the relationship between provision of library service and learning outcomes for students.

The first phase of the evaluation was to establish base line information about resource centre programs. The second phase was to examine variations among programs and to assess their relative impact on schools. When dollars are devoted to school library services, is there corresponding value for students? There were two areas to explore: the role of teacher-librarians and the skill level and attitudes of students. To address the first area, a committee composed of the school principal, teacher-librarian, and two teachers in each school responded to the Liesener Inventory of Services.[2]

The Liesener Inventory was selected not only because it has been extensively field tested, but also because it stands as a major authoritative instrument in school library evaluation. This inventory is a refinement of the Gaver Inventory administered in Calgary in 1971. The inventory was used to describe the breadth of the resource centre program through a description of its events. District staff personally administered each inventory to ensure consistent interpretation at a regularly controlled pace.

A locally developed attitude measure was designed to determine students' feelings about their resource centres through responses to items such as:

Item 14: "The library is a favourite place of mine in the school."

An elementary school research skills test was developed locally, based on the district's scope and sequence research chart. It was subsequently pilot tested on two elementary schools that were not to be participants in the research project. A senior high school research skills test was based on a test developed and field tested by a committee of school and district personnel.

For both attitude and skill measures, two Year Six classes and two Year Twelve classes were tested in each school, except in small elementary schools where there was only one Year Six class available. In each case, the tests were administered by district staff.

The above measures were used to gather quantitative data which was then coupled with qualitative data gleaned from all of the schools sampled. This was done through detailed observation in a wide variety of school resource centres using goal-free observation techniques such as those described by Barry MacDonald at the University of East Anglia[3] and Elliot Eisner.[4] An important consideration was that the past observations of the library media consultants could not be relied upon because those observations tended to be biased, as visits usually occurred on an individual basis.

Each case study involved a two-day observation period using unobtrusive observational techniques and interviews with students, classroom teachers, library/media staff and administrators. As the case studies progressed, it became obvious that background variables other than those described in the Liesener Inventory needed to be taken into account. These variables might enable, or limit, the capacity of the resource centre to provide the services listed in the Liesener Inventory.

The Liesener Inventory of Library Services includes items related to the existence of various types of library material, access to library production services, in-library instruction services and consulting services, contribution to school curriculum and teacher instruction.

Student skills and attitudes include library access skills, general book knowledge, instrumental value of the library to school work, and positive sentiment towards the library.

Background characteristics include personal qualifications of the teacher-librarian (e.g., education, seniority, teaching experience), size of the library program (e.g., time entitlement, library budget), size of the school (e.g., enrollment, budget), consultant visits, educational ability (e.g., student verbal and nonverbal, level of education in the immediate neighborhood), and others such as seniority of the principal and age of the school.

Analysis of the extensive data collected was directed by Dr. W. J. Reeves of the University of Calgary Sociology Department. His involvement as a methodologist was crucial to the project. A multivariate regression analysis was conducted to determine relationships between the objective data and background characteristics. With a possibility of approximately 30,000 correlations, this aspect of the evaluation project demanded the full capacity of the district computer. Only those findings that could be confirmed in both statistical and observational data are reported and, of these, only findings which can be supported by correlation of .6 and more are included.

FINDINGS

At the first level of research findings, this study has confirmed what resource centres in Calgary look like. It is now known that even the basic core services offer support for teachers, opportunities for students, and a variety of general services including instruction for children. These "Baseline Library Services" do not, in and of themselves, represent an ideal nor complete program. What is amazing, however, is that in spite of dramatically different conditions in schools, resource centres are able to offer a broad list of common services.

When a service was offered in all or almost all schools, it was considered a program norm or part of a core of services offered throughout the district. Approximately fifty-five baseline services were offered by all resource centres. In addition, approximately thirty baseline services were offered by all or almost all elementary schools. Similarly, approximately thirty different baseline services were unique to senior high resource centres.

Core Services were clustered into four areas. Because the configuration was different at the elementary and senior high levels, they were labelled differently. The similarity of focus is, however, readily apparent.

BASELINE LIBRARY SERVICES

Elementary Schools	High Schools
The Child's Domain	Individual Instruction for Students
Reference Services for Individual Teachers	Group Instruction for Students
General Use Services	Teacher Services
	Library Administration

In the elementary school, the Child's Domain encompassed a variety of awareness and guidance services regarding resources.

Students had a wide variety of materials to choose from, in a variety of locations, and they were also alerted by the resource centre staff to materials and services in the library. Once students were cognizant of the existence of materials, they also received assistance from the teacher-librarian in locating and selecting materials most appropriate to their interests and needs. Renewal procedures were available in all elementary schools, should the student require this service. It was apparent that individuals and small groups of students used the library if the need arose in the classroom; in fact, small groups were regularly sent to the library to work with the teacher-librarian on assignments. Audio-visual equipment was available as required.

Student instruction occupied a large amount of resource centre staff time. Formal instructional program activities were evident in all elementary libraries. Individual instruction and guidance was offered to all students in all elementary schools, on request. This instruction occurred in the areas of reference materials and skills, research skills and the use and handling of audio-visual equipment.

Services clustered under the label "general use" in the elementary school centered around management of the library facility, collection and equipment, and awareness activities directed toward special events such as Book Week.

In the senior high schools, library administration was directed toward improving access to materials, including reservation systems and interlibrary loans.

Having identified the constants regarding school library programs in the district, it was noted that the role of school librarian as teacher and resource specialist was implicit. At this stage of the analysis only those items that varied in the sample (that is, where approximately half the sampled schools said "Yes!" and half said "No!" to the item) were investigated. Given the theoretical model of the research, it was important to know if it made a difference to the students whether the school had a particular library service or not—were the students in approximately half the schools who said "Yes" to a Liesener item more skillful or more positive than the students in the other schools who said "No!" From another perspective, was the existence or absence of a library service determined in any way by the background characteristics of the librarian, library, or school?

Examination of services which were found to be provided in some schools, and not in others, revealed an expanded role for the teacher-librarian. This role is one of school-based consultant, with an additional program component dealing with audio-visual services. These two elements of consultation and audio-visual service manifest themselves differently at the elementary and senior high levels. Nevertheless, the pattern of development relative to individual schools and the district at large was remarkably consistent.

ELEMENTARY SCHOOLS

Initially, cooperation between teachers and teacher-librarians led to the selection of resources for teacher use *or* to extend and enrich experiences for students. At the next level, both these elements were present. A further stage of development was found when classroom teachers and the teacher-librarian engaged in a form of team teaching. In this case, the approach was frequently a division of labor, with the teacher-librarian entering the instructional sequence based on expertise. For example, instruction in the use of biographical reference works might be designed into a social studies unit. Fully developed consultation occurred when classroom teachers and the teacher-librarian planned an instructional sequence, conducted instruction cooperatively and shared in student and program evaluation. Approximately 20 percent of the schools exhibited this level of development.

CONSULTATION INDEX LEVEL

Consultation leading to team lesson planning, and teaching cooperatively   5

Consultation leading to team teaching with classroom teacher   4

Consultation leading to selection of resources for teacher use AND for enrichment of student programs   3

Consultation leading to selection of resources for teacher OR for enrichment of student programs   2

No consultation with teams of teachers

Along with the consultative role of the teacher-librarian, the production of instructional materials was found to be a critical variable. This service element was not, at the time of the study, well developed. Typically, the library staff provided a video tape dubbing service for teachers.

It was important to consider what characteristics were related to whether or not the expanded role of the school library was present in elementary schools. Those with background and experience in libraries will not be surprised that the relationship was one of time (providing sufficient time for the teacher-librarian to work in the program) and money (providing sufficient funds in the library budget). What was gratifying about this finding, was the strength of the relationship and the precision with which we could establish cut points regarding variables. Because there was not a perfect relationship between school size and the amount of teacher-librarian time, some relatively small schools were able to exhibit the two variables and some large schools did not. Systematically, however, in small schools with less than half-time teacher-librarians and larger schools with less than two thirds of the teacher-librarian's time deployed to the program, the consultative role and production service was absent. Admittedly "small" and "larger" applied to school size are defined differently. At the time of the study, 14 elementary schools had enrollments of less than 150 students and the average size of school was nine classrooms. In addition, every school library has clerical staff and is supported by centralized ordering, cataloguing, processing, and a variety of school-directed services.

Similarly, data analysis revealed that, in terms of 1978 dollars, any school library budget which was less than $2,500 for materials, systematically exhibited no consultative or production role. Of particular interest was a further systematic relationship between the amount of time devoted to the school by library media consultants and production. When there had been five or more visits to the school, there was a strong positive relationship to the presence of the expanded role. This finding inspires much speculation and is deserving of more attention than can be paid in this article.

What about student outcomes in terms of skills and attitudes? Certainly, there were some items that stood out as bearing a strong relationship to the sentiments and skill development of children. For example, there was .8 correlation between the housing of photographs in the library and children declaring that the library was the most interesting place in the school. An interesting phenomenon, but hardly a significant one in the overall scheme of things. An equally strong relationship was one of socioeconomic status (SES) of the neighborhood to the importance which students assigned to the library. In lower SES schools, children systematically indicated that the library was important to their success in school. The reverse was also true; and this phenomenon was also related to the way the library was scheduled and the specific skills that were acquired.

The observational data collected during the case studies, together with the strong results regarding consultation, confirmed that the "first" clients of the elementary school library were the teachers who, in turn, sponsored children individually or in small and large groups to go to the library. Because the library program does not, nor can be expected to, have a mandated curriculum, the inconclusive results of skill measures were not surprising. There was, however, strong positive effect upon students' attitudes when teacher-librarians performed a consultative role with teachers. When this full partnership occurred, as was the case in 5 of the sampled schools, there was an obvious coordination and integration of the library program with classroom activities. Typically, the teacher-librarians in these schools were involved at the initial planning stages of the project, took part in cooperative or team teaching activities as the project progressed, and were certainly engaged in evaluation and follow-up at the project's conclusion.

In regard to the testing procedures, no attempt was made to test for library skill ability in subject areas, nor was performance testing carried out due to constraints of time. What is known, however, is that in schools where consultation did occur, library skills per se were not generally taught as a separate curriculum area, but instruction appeared to be given as the need arose in the classroom and after careful consultation between teacher and teacher-librarian. Furthermore, because only Grade 6 students were tested and knowing that teachers sponsor their classes to the library, it was not possible that the classes tested had not yet been sponsored for instruction in the skills that were being tested. Ideally, the entire school population should have been tested and those results examined in light of students being sponsored or non-sponsored to the library. The effects of the library program upon students is indirect, and is dependent upon teachers sponsoring student use of the services and resources that are resident in the resource program.

SENIOR HIGH SCHOOLS

Relationships between school library program development and student outcomes was more conclusive at the senior high school. In the area of extended library services, the elementary beginnings come to fruition at the secondary level. The continued importance of time in regards to consultation between teacher and teacher-librarian is, further, more specifically identifiable at high school to include the effects of specific kinds of consultation on student skills and attitudes.

Similarly, the audio-visual component which has its beginnings in the expanded teacher-librarian role at the elementary level, through the production of instructional materials for teachers, matures at the secondary level through more extensive audio-visual services.

In senior high, the expanded role can be obtained only when there is an adequate library budget and adequate clerical time which in turn manifests itself in two major areas inside the expanded role: the audio-visual component and differentiated consultative services. The audio-visual component, which includes services such as photography, has a significant impact on student attitudes.

At the secondary level, the existence and type of consultation are heavily dependent on how much clerical time is resident in the program. Since all senior high teacher-librarians work on a full-time basis, the operant variable, therefore, became the number of clerical staff and/or the amount of time spent in the program by the clerical assistant(s). This was a refinement in terms of the elementary program where not every teacher-librarian was able to devote full-time to the library program and his/her time then became the operant variable. In addition, at the secondary level, given an adequate number of clerical assistants, the resource centre was able to act as a media clearinghouse, and became involved in student-oriented consultation as well as in specific classroom projects.

Consultation was manifested in different ways, each of these having a strong positive relationship to specific student skills and sentiments. For example, when a classroom teacher and teacher-librarian cooperatively developed alternative learning situations for students (student-oriented consultation), the students systematically responded that the library staff was helpful and that the library was the most interesting place in the school. When team teaching occurred as a result of consultation, student reference skills were high. In the case of these items, the range of student scores by school was 30 percent to 78 percent on the administered skills test.

High scoring schools typically exhibited team teaching consultative behaviors. The range of student scores in the area of research skills, that is knowledge of how to begin a research project, was 47 percent to 80 percent. High scoring schools typically provided audio-visual services and the teacher-librarian was involved in developing and implementing class projects.

When school libraries provided extended audio-visual services, including listing, stocking and evaluating nonprint materials, and provision for photography, students systematically reported positive sentiments toward the library. These were manifested in students declaring that the school library was important to their success in school, that they used the library outside of class time, and that they used the library even when this was not required for assignments.

The presence of the audio-visual component was, as one might expect, strongly related to significantly higher expenditure on nonprint materials. In these schools, students placed more instrumental value on the school library (it is important to my success in school) and exhibited higher scores in research skills. Interestingly, the presence of selection services in the area of nonprint was related to significantly higher expenditure on periodicals.

Consultation, particularly with regard to team teaching and the presence of a clearinghouse function, dealing with the widest range of school resources, was related to higher expenditure on books and the presence of two or more clerks. The number of clerks required to have an impact on this type of consultation varied directly with the size of the school.

LEADING EDGE PROGRAMS

When a service was offered by only a few schools, this service was at the "leading edge." These program elements are considered to be important in the field of school librarianship and may be common in other districts, but at this time, in Calgary schools, represented program extensions.

Examples of leading edge services included computer applications, identification of student learning styles and cooperatively developed resource centre goal and budget statements. However, this role was not well-defined at the time of the study. It is hoped that as programs progress, there will be a "collapsing towards the middle" whereby those services presently considered leading edge will move into the area of variable services and some of the variable services will shift into the area of core services. There had been some confirmation in this regard, available only one year later, in the area of microcomputers.

SUMMARY

The overall finding that important program elements have direct positive impact upon the students and that sufficient resources must be present in order for this to occur, will be no surprise to those intimately familiar with school libraries. As is always the case, the process of data gathering and analysis was, in itself, beneficial and stimulated some important activities. The Chief Superintendent accepted the conclusion that the Calgary Board of Education was receiving value for dollar in the areas of teacher support and positive student outcomes.

It is said that good research raises more questions than it provides answers. Many surprises were found and these bear further scrutiny. Among these are:

1. The training and background of the teacher-librarian was unrelated to the extent of the program or to student outcomes.

2. Verbal ability of students and socioeconomic status of the neighborhood was not related to the presence of extended services or positive student outcomes.

3. The Liesener Inventory is based on the assumption that "more is better." There are, clearly, some services that are more important than others. Indeed, the provision of some services was found to have a *negative* correlation with student outcomes!

CONCLUSIONS

Analysis of the findings yielded four major conclusions:

1. Library programs are an integrative resource in schools. Successful programs involve the teaching staff, school administrators, and central office functions.

2. The inconsistent deployment of staff time and materials budgets results in uneven program implementation from school to school. It appears that this inconsistency is related to administrative support and the teaching styles prevalent within the school.

3. The resource centre program is unlike a curriculum. Rather, it is a service that must be entrenched in the total school program, if students and teachers are to receive maximum benefits. When the program is dealt with as a residual of school resources, there is little provided that is meaningful for its clients.

4. Some schools do not have the necessary resources to support quality library programs without severely penalizing a curriculum area.

REFERENCES

1. Calgary Board of Education. *School Library Program Evaluation*. Office of the Chief Superintendent, Calgary Board of Education, 1981.

2. Liesener, James W. "The Development of a Planning Process for Media Programs," *School Media Quarterly*, I (Summer, 1973), pp. 278-87.

Liesener, James W. *Planning Instruments for School Library Media Programs*. American Library Association, 1974.

Liesener, James W. *A Systematic Process for Planning Media Programs*. American Library Association, 1976.

3. MacDonald, Barry. *Evaluation and the Control of Education*. Ford Foundation Safari Project. University of East Anglia: Centre for Applied Research in Education, 1974 (mimeographed).

4. Eisner, Eliot W. *The Perceptive Eye: Toward the Reformation of Educational Evaluation*. Paper presented at the meeting of the American Educational Research Association Division B, Curriculum and Objectives. Washington, D.C., March 31st, 1973.

Research on Library Services for Children and Young Adults: Implications for Practice

Shirley Fitzgibbons

INTRODUCTION

During the 1970s, there has been a great deal of "gnashing of teeth" over the scarcity of research concerning children and young adult services in public libraries by those who have attempted state of the art reviews of research (Gallivan, 1974;[1] Shontz, 1982[2]); and those who have written about the importance and need for such research (Billeter, 1975;[3] Kingsbury, 1977;[4] Fasick, 1978;[5] Lukenbill, 1979;[6] Furman, 1979;[7] and Fitzgibbons, 1980[8]). Gallivan in her review of research published from 1960-1972 identified only fourteen studies on public library service concerning the preschool age group through age fourteen. She recognized that school libraries have far more frequently been the object of research than public libraries, identifying thirty-two such studies for her review. There are also several outstanding reviews of school

library research: Gaver (for the period up to 1960, 1962, 1969)[9] Lowrie (1950-1967 period, 1968);[10] Aaron (1967-1971, 1972);[11] Barron (1972-1976, 1977)[12] and Aaron (1977-1980, 1982).[13] Kingsbury[14] identified six studies concerning public library services, in addition to the Gallivan group. Shontz, looking only at research related to children and young adult services in public libraries both before 1970 (earliest study was 1941) and after that date, summarized forty studies specifically designed to study some aspect of public library service to children and young adults, thirty of these studies lamenting the lack of research. This paper will suggest that it is possible to draw implications from the best major studies and from groups of small-scale studies.

It is unlikely that the 1980s will produce a greater amount of research concerning services to children and young adults, due to governmental and institutional budget problems.

Service practitioners are fighting for their jobs, and for maintaining even traditional services. It is for these reasons that it is all the more important for those concerned about the future of these services to examine closely what we already know from research and to try to use this knowledge in practice. The cry has been sounded for the need for hard facts to justify services and staff; for the skills of measurement and evaluation in planning and evaluating continuing and new services; and for knowing the processes for establishing goals and setting priorities. What does research since 1970 tell practitioners?

WHAT IS RESEARCH?

Before one can even suggest that a particular study or a group of studies provide evidence to consider in decision-making, it is important to explore briefly the definition of research. In the broadest framework, there are at least two types of research, basic and applied. More recently, a concept labeled either locally-based research, field research, evaluation research, or action research appears in library literature, as a part of the applied research area. Even though the area of basic research is fundamental to the furthering of knowledge in terms of theory building and testing, practitioners are most concerned with applied, and most specifically with field, research which helps to clarify practices and evaluate particular techniques and services in specific settings.

As in most areas of librarianship, research concerning services to children and young adults tends to be survey or historical, is usually noncumulative, and tends to be unsophisticated in terms of statistical techniques. Rather than be deterred by the state of the art, we will examine the best of the major studies which address fundamental problems facing services in the 1980s. Research concerning materials, such as content analysis, though pertinent for collection development, will not be included, as it is discussed sufficiently elsewhere. There will be no attempt either to review the studies qualitatively nor to discuss methodology, both of which are found in review articles. References will lead the reader directly to the research report, reviews, and/or popular journal articles. References include citations to all sources available, or to only one when that is the most accessible. No attempt has been made to undertake an exhaustive research literature search, rather those studies already identified in literature available to practitioners and researchers will be the focus.

WHAT RESEARCH CAN AND CANNOT DO

Kingsbury argues that research "...can win support since the force of evidence is often necessary to convince people of the value of children's services."[4:132] Fasick points out that "...(research) cannot answer questions of value, cannot tell you what your goals should be, but only indicate how you might achieve particular goals."[5:345] Though this is generally true, a Delphi study by Kingsbury (1978)[14,15] does identify goals (trends and innovations) of national leaders of children's services. Simplistic suggestions may result from studies that do not fully take in consideration the many variables that may affect a particular research question. However, when study after study shows similar results, it is apparent that something is generally true. Fasick suggests, "Research, in the broad meaning of a careful, systematic search for new facts, should help in the task of measuring and evaluating children's services, but it is not a panacea that will solve all library problems.[5:344]

Though not correctly labeled research, the use of statistical information is important as Winnick so clearly emphasized, "Without national evaluative studies or quantitative standards for measuring public library service to children, the use of recurring statistical information could illuminate the condition and document the development of these services."[16] She went on to say that statistics have not been collected systematically in the past, either at the national level, by state record keeping, or at local levels. A great deal of information is available today, and can be used to identify users/nonusers and needs in the local community. Practitioners need to locate this data and use it wisely.

ACCESS TO RESEARCH

Much dissertation research never becomes published as a monograph, and many of them never appear in journal articles. This is a problem that should be addressed elsewhere; but it seems important to point out an apparent bias among scholarly journals in the library/information field concerning research in the children and young adult services area. Also, our own professional journals have not been particularly research conscious until quite recently; the editors of those journals seem to want the content of the studies to be "popularized" and made "good reading" to the point that there is often little substance available to judge the quality of the research being presented, or to assess the methods and techniques to determine its generalizability and importance.

In the interim, this brief article will look at major research studies that apply to public library services to children and young adults and will tentatively make suggestions concerning what we can learn from this research.

IMPLICATIONS

Shontz, in her review of the forty studies of some aspect of public library service to children and young adults, presented five examples of generalizations from recent research which have implications for decision-making in public libraries:

> Public library use studies report high use of the public library collection and services by young adults, and young adults' preference for using the public library over the school library. (Yet young adult services and programs are not given high priority.)

> Storytelling services and summer reading clubs have apparent positive effects on children's learning. (Yet these programs are sometimes overlooked by administrators, and suffer from budget cutting.)

A lack of qualified personnel is a crucial problem in the development of library programs for children and young adults. (Yet few library schools have responded to the need for specialized education programs in early childhood education and young adult programing).

Younger children and children from lower socio-economic levels have a greater need for audio-visual materials. (Yet public libraries have been slow in developing multimedia services for children).

Schools and public libraries serve essentially the same children and have many common goals, and purposes. There are benefits to each from sharing knowledge, collections, and services. (Yet it is obvious that they are not communicating or cooperating with each other in promoting learning in children).

The rest of this article will group the studies under the following categories of research: goals and future outlook; state-wide surveys; administrative studies; reading interests, behaviour and motivations; use and user studies; school/public library cooperation; programming and services—general, and services to special groups (early childhood, special children, young adults); professional image of youth librarians.

Goals and Future Outlook

Two studies serving similar purposes are those by Kingsbury[14,15] for children's services and Downen (1979)[17] for young adult services. Both use modified Delphi techniques, and assess perceptions of persons who are usually in decision-making positions. Kingsbury queried the coordinators of children's services concerning trends, goals, and innovations in children's services over the next twenty-five years. Downen asked directors of public library systems (serving at least 100,000 people) to list the most important developments they would either expect or would like to see initiated in public libraries' programs for young adults over the following fifteen years. Kingsbury found two priorities evident on the part of respondents: children's librarians must become truly adminis-trators (act as part of the planning team); and they must provide services to those not already served by the public library to ensure the survival of children's services (pre-schoolers, exceptional children, and those indifferent to school). Some of these goals have since been implemented in many public libraries; all should consider them.

Downen found it highly encouraging that an over-whelming majority (81 percent) of the survey respondents felt that service to young adults should be continued and expanded; though 47 percent of these respondents were uncer-tain whether or not this would still be the case by the year 1993. Even though 66 percent felt it undesirable that the YA department be eliminated, 36 percent were uncertain regarding the probability. He concluded that though directors show uncertainty as to the future of YA services, they do feel it is important and a desirable function of the public library. He also pointed out reactions to alternatives to a discrete YA department: negative feelings toward placing it with the juvenile department, positive feelings of putting YA services into the adult department; and/or making it a broader area such as adult services or readers advisory. There was less emphasis on programs and more on reading and orientation toward general education/motivation for lifetime use of libraries. There was great uncertainty regarding increased bibliotherapeutic use of materials and training of the YA librarian as a quasi-counselor.

State-wide Surveys of Children's Services

The 1970s have produced several major statewide surveys of children's (sometimes including young adult) services in public libraries, including North Carolina (1972),[18] New York (1972),[19] Illinois (1978),[20] Ohio (1979),[21] Wisconsin (1980),[22] and California (1981).[23] The major studies have usually been done in cooperation with a library school or research center, the state library association's children (and/or young adults) section, and/or the state library agency and have often had funding. Recent studies easily found in the literature to date are those of Illinois,[20] Ohio[21] and Wisconsin.[22] The studies seem to be done for a similar reason: to serve as status quo descriptions of service to the specific age group as it exists in the state; sometimes they use a sampling of libraries, all libraries, and/or recommended "exemplary" libraries.

Results show similarities such as the Wisconsin study report indication of major inequities in the lack of propor-tionate relationship between the percent of children's materials circulated and the budget, staff, and space alloted to them. The proportion of circulation of children and young adult materials was at least 40 percent in two-fifths of these libraries; and more than 50 percent in 15 percent of them. Equally distressing was the fact that only about half of the libraries involved their children's staff in areas of library decision-making (budget, personnel, goals). The Illinois study showed similar results to Wisconsin's with the mean percentage of total library expenditures spent on children's services at 25 percent, while the mean percentage of library circulation in children's services at 34 percent. The lack of initiative on the part of children's librarians to concern themselves with budget decisions was again mentioned, with many librarians having their first exposure to the library's annual report through the study. Fasick points out these anomalies which invite further investigation and discussion: the overwhelming rejection of suggestions to eliminate children's services coupled with a lack of interest in measurement or evaluation of these services; the apparent lack of understanding of the nature and purpose of setting library goals; the high priority given to the presentation of film programs while at the same time a lack of concern for film as a medium of artistic expression.

The Connecticut Research Documentation Project, initiated by Hektoen and as reported (1980, 1981),[24] seems to be more of a systematic gathering of statistics on an ongoing basis in order to better describe current services than research; but it's a very important effort at developing measurement instruments after deciding what measurements were needed, and how and by whom the data could best be gathered to record use of the public library's children's services. Generalizations such as Connecticut libraries do not have enough children's materials, and that elementary school libraries lack both materials and professionally trained librarians led to the obvious suggestion for closer work with schools. The many community service referral questions, and increased adult use of children's services indicated that there is an increasing new client group for children's librarians—the adult who works with children.

Starr and Talbot[25] surveyed the post-Proposition 13 status of public library services for children and young adults in California as compared to before Proposition 13. Though their response rate was poor with almost no response from school libraries, almost an equal number of children and young adult public librarians responded. A dismal picture was presented with decreases in hours, staff, in-service training, programs, etc.; but the point of the survey was to urge Californians to "use the cold figures ... provide ammunition for those who wish to fight the battle for quality library service."[25] This seems to be a valid rationale for such a study; however these results should continue to be monitored in terms of services and efforts of professionals and interested publics in that state. Could Massachusetts or other states with similar problems be helped by the California experience?

Administrative Studies

A national study by Benne (1978, 1980)[26] tried to identify the roles and functions of central children's libraries in urban library systems in terms of the changes in cities, the changes in administrative patterns, and the priorities set in response to financial problems. Benne did not attempt to judge the quality of effectiveness of services in this exploratory survey. She found a great deal of isolation on the part of these children's librarians (not participating in departmental meetings, or on committees); the number of professional positions had decreased (more than half reported a decrease), and that qualifications had been changed (lowered) so that less occupants have the MLS degree. In a time when hours had been decreased, more than one-half the circulation from the children's collection in the central library occurs on weekends. She suggested that many problems seem to stem from a mutual misunderstanding of roles (rather than as personality differences).

It was further suggested that children's services staff seem to place a higher priority on the education role rather than the information/reference role. This includes the adult public who needs help with children's materials or programming and uses the children's literature collection frequently as a reference source. Adult publics were identified as those concerned mainly with the child and those concerned with children's literature. User groups were ranked in the following order: school aged children, preschool children, parents, and adult users of children's literature. Benne felt the educational role assumption needs to be explored more fully.

Reading Interests, Behavior, Motivation

Most reading interest studies fall into simple surveys of favorite titles, or types of books, are studies of one city or large public library system, or of one state, and seem to be mainly directed toward young adults (Goetze, 1972;[27] Hutchinson, 1973;[28] Campbell et al, 1974;[29] Alm, 1974;[30] Wynn and Newmark, 1979[31]). It is surprising how similar the top ten lists are, whether by title, author, or subject during any time period, and despite the variety of geographical areas. These results are interesting for other libraries to consider; and more importantly, to undertake similar surveys, using the same techniques and age groups.

The most recent survey by Wynn and Newmark pointed out the importance of local surveys and some of the benefits that can result: an increased cooperation between the public library and the school (administrators, teachers, and librarians) based on the cooperative effort of the survey as well as some of the specific results; information for collection development to better meet current interests and needs of a user group; and information on specific service areas improvement. The time spent on the survey could be easily justified due to these results. The learning and discussion as a part of the process with those people who should be talking with each other is an important by product of research.

One study, though limited to high school students in one city (Carlson, et al, 1975)[32] has become an annual survey, and appears regularly in *English Journal*. It is especially useful in showing trends and changes over time. Another area study which has now been accomplished three times is the Bay Area Young Adult Librarians (BAYA) survey which also shows changes over time of enduring topics, authors, and specific titles. (Minudri and Bodart, 1973,[33] 1975; Bodart, 1979.)[34] In the most recent study, it was found that four authors (Tolkien, Hinton, Zindel, and Asimov) appeared for the first time, with two of her titles appearing, but was only popular with the younger teens. Fantasy, and escapist fiction (love, mysteries, and adventure) rated the highest. Surprisingly, paperbacks were not as highly preferred as expected, especially among older teens; and TV and movies though still an influence did not specifically influence as many choices as previously.

Two national studies of reading interests of teenagers (Freiberger, 1973;[35] Stachelek, 1977[36]) show similar results as the local studies for similar time periods, giving a great deal of credibility to generalization from local studies. In 1973, it was found that major interests were the occult and supernatural, fantasy and science fiction and problem young adult fiction. In 1977, science fiction, romance and stories about teens endured as well as the escapist literature mentioned by the BAYA poll. Among these twelfth graders, however, paperbacks were still preferred. Generally, half of these students were moderate readers, while one-third identified themselves as avid readers (a higher percentage than usual).

A more indepth study by Greenberg (1979)[37] studied the factors that led seventh grade students to choose books. Factors contributing included: family participation and encouragement; a school library, librarian, and teachers that rewarded reading ability; friends that viewed reading positively; a public library and librarian that promoted good relations with the students; and a family income that afforded comic books, magazines, and books. Students read on the basis of personal recommendations, printed recommendations, and by the subject, title, cover, and display of the material. There are implications here for collection development, suggested topics and titles for booktalks and displays, and for librarians being willing to share books and to create a reading environment.

Many of the reading surveys could and did include questions about use of libraries, sources of books and other information, and reading patterns. Numerous studies exist in the reading field in this area—with similar results to many of the library studies. For example, Scharf (1973)[38] examined reading habits in relation to sex, grade level, and intelligence. Students with higher IQs read more. Seniors read more materials regularly, prefer public libraries to school libraries, and prefer paperback books.

Somewhat similar was the Doyen study (1980)[39] which tried to compare reading preferences of different student groups, an inner city black junior high population with an alternative racially balanced school for the creative and performing arts. Two constants were the collection and the librarians; and by comparing the circulation figures, Doyen concluded that contrary to popular assumption, large discrepancies in reading patterns did not exist. The main difference found was that the students from the alternative arts environment read more fiction and had a positive attitude toward leisure-time reading. That the school curriculum may be less important than other factors is interesting; and needs to be explored further by both school and public librarians. From reading studies, indications that home influences, reading ability and peer influences are most important also need to be considered. Bard and Leide[40] compared reading interests of grades one to six. While boys and girls began as first graders preferring imaginative literature; boys by the third grade preferred nonfiction, an interest which continued through sixth grade. By the fifth grade, girls preferred realistic fiction. Sex and age differences were certainly apparent. Do librarians consider these differences as they make booklists, booktalks, and encourage the reading of quality literature?

Media influences and effects are also important for public librarians working with children and young adults. Fasick (1970)[41] compared language in books and television to determine language learning from the two media. She found that children do not appear to learn as much language (verbal skills) from television as compared with being read picture books. As she points out, more research is needed to compare the differing effects of use of the two media; however, this is an excellent rationale for targeting the preschooler and the early primary child in story hour programs with parent involvement so that reading aloud will be continued in the home environment in place of some of the many hours now spent by this age group on watching television. Film preferences of fourth and fifth graders were studied by Cox (1975)[42] in terms of differences related to sex, race, or socioeconomic status. Boys and girls' ranking were nearly identical except boys like a type labeled action/sport/outdoors while girls like a fantasy/excitement type. There were not significant differences between sex, race or socioeconomic status; however, all children showed a preference for certain film form/techniques such as narrative/live-action; narrative/animation; and liking least non-narrative/animation films. Film selections are an important part of both collection building and programming for children and young adults and an area we need to know more about.

Use and User Studies

This one area alone could comprise this entire article but an attempt will be made to highlight the results of important studies. Several early studies need to be reviewed as base line data in interpreting the results of more recent use studies in establishing how many of the total users are youth, types of uses, total percentage of circulation of youth groups, and user profile characteristics. Two major urban public library studies by Martin (1967, 1969)[43] indicated that the young adult age group was one of the largest user groups, even though the library made only limited provision for them. In Chicago in 1969, 57.8 percent of young adults in the city were public library users; and over one-third of the users of the adult section of the library were from fifteen to nineteen years old. In an even earlier study, looking only at students in Baltimore (1963),[44] it was found that two-thirds of all high school students read an average of six books per month for school work; that school libraries did not have that substantial a subject collection; and young adults preferred to use the public library over their school libraries. This same finding is echoed in more recent studies. Wilder (1970)[45] in examining library usage by students in five Indiana cities discovered students found the public library more useful in school-related terms than school libraries and regarded public librarians more favorably. Even though Wilder found elementary aged children made up only ten percent of public library patrons, they used it with the greatest frequency and ninety-five percent were satisfied with the services.

Benford (1969, 1971)[46] reported on the now well-known Philadelphia Project which included a major survey of students in grades two through twelve in Philadelphia's public, parochial, and independent schools. Though this study is now over ten years old, many earlier and later small scale studies corroborate the findings. The rather startling news at that time was the change in attitude toward school libraries and public libraries often taking place between the fourth and twelfth grades with accompanying use patterns. While 61 percent of the fourth graders enjoyed reading to fulfill teachers' assignments, only 22 percent of the twelfth graders do; a drop in enjoyment of recreational reading is also evident with 75 percent of students in the fourth and sixth grades enjoying such reading as compared to 62 percent of the twelfth graders. In terms of use of libraries, 42 percent of sixth and twelfth graders used both school and public libraries, while 13 percent used only school libraries, 13 percent only public libraries, and 13 percent depended solely on other sources. The percent of students who only use the public library increases from 5 percent in the sixth grade to 21 percent in the twelfth grade. While half the students using libraries say they are satisfied, others complain about inability to find books they can read, failure to get assistance from library staff, negative feeling toward too many rules and regulations, etc. The negative feelings increase from more than half of elementary students finding nothing dissatisfying about their libraries to two-thirds of the twelfth graders dissatisfied with school libraries (50 percent of them like everything about the public library).

Tower (1972)[47] in a study of changes in children's library services in Pittsburgh suburbs for the 1960-1970 period, found that as population increased, quality improved (resources, staff, budgets). School libraries showed greater change, due to federal funds and a Pennsylvania state mandate.

In an indepth analysis of fifth grader user and nonuser attitudes toward school and public libraries, Ekechukwu (1972)[48] discovered that there was a significant relationship between attitudes toward public libraries and use. Though a greater number were users of school libraries (which would be expected), a greater percentage of fifth graders had more favorable attitudes toward public libraries. They used libraries mainly for the book collection (of both libraries) for the books to read outside the library and secondly, for school-related purposes. They most disliked the rules and regulations. Though sex was not a significant variable in terms of library use, girls had more favorable attitudes than boys toward public libraries. Apparently, negative attitudes toward school libraries began even before the junior high setting. None of these studies tried to analyze the reasons why student users formed such negative attitudes toward school libraries as compared to public libraries.

Fasick and England (1977)[49] investigated how well the collection and services of a Canadian public library met the educational and recreational needs of children from six to twelve years of age. More than 90 percent viewed the book collection as the major attraction; with nonprint drawing 15 percent and programs, 15 percent. Though the most frequently mentioned reason for using the library was to select books for personal reading, differences between boys and girls were apparent; boys were more likely than girls to come for informational purposes (both school and own interests). The use of library materials for school projects increases with age, and more so for boys. Implications for collection building are obvious; with circulation of fiction three times greater than nonfiction while only about 50 percent of the collection was fiction. About one child in eight expressed an interest in library programs, with film shows the most popular type.

User satisfaction was expressed in terms of finding what they were looking for with access through the catalogue though there are fewer subject headings than desired; boys offer more suggestions for changes and materials than girls. Nonusers did not present major differences as a group though school children who were interviewed in the school and classified as school users (as compared to the public library users) read less books and newspapers, had less ambitious career and educational aspirations, and had less positive self-images. Both groups viewed television frequently, enjoying the same kinds of programs, and in terms of books, both preferred fiction, especially mysteries, adventure, and horror stories. An implication of this study is that due to the similarity of users and nonusers, nonusers might be encouraged to use the library without any dramatic changes in collections or programs. One idea is to promote more nonbook materials for those who do not read for pleasure. Less than 7 percent of any group named the school library as their first information source; and when asked where they would turn first for information, one half of the school sample named a person (parent, teacher, friend) with almost 40 percent of the library sample doing the same. However, more than one-third think

of the library as a source of information. Sex differences were greater than user/nonuser differences for those under nine. As Fasick pointed out in her study, there is little information available about the factors which lead one child to use the public library while another does not; in 1965, Parker[50] had indicated that the adult user variables that characterize use (such as age, sex, ethnic and language background, and socio-economic class) do not seem to relate to children as a user group. This needs to be more fully studied.

The access question is explored by Moll (1975)[51] who found that for children reading above national norms, the subject catalogs provided access to 70 percent of the juvenile books, but that only 28 percent of children's books were accessible if national findings regarding children's reading levels were applied. This conclusion that the subject card catalog does not provide effective access to information for children is disconcerting in terms of Fasick indicating that children access the collection generally through the catalogue. An interesting perspective was presented by Fasick (1978, 1979)[52] in her comparison study of views on services of librarians, parents, and teachers. Generally there was agreement on traditional services such as librarians guiding children in book selection; in developing a love for reading, and providing story hour programs, as well as the newer idea of providing experiences for children under three. Priority differences in services and programs were indicated by parents and teachers rating as higher priorities, interlibrary loans, joint programs for parents and children, and providing a place for children to meet friends; with librarians preferring as priorities helping parents choose books for children, and allowing children to use the adult section. In terms of collection development issues, parents and teachers felt more favorably toward series books and books based on popular TV series, audiovisual materials/and hardware, with librarians preferring comic books and sex education materials, and the groups agreeing on poetry, classical music, and popular recordings, toys for preschoolers, and games for children to use in the library. As one of the only studies of this type, it would be an interesting experience for local libraries to replicate in their community to help reach some consensus as a group on types of materials bought and types of programs sponsored with public monies.

A citation analysis of high school students' term papers by Mancall (1978, 1979)[53] indicated interesting implications for collection building in school and public libraries, as well as for library instruction. Students depended heavily on monographs, rather than journals or other media; references were surprisingly old; and patterns of use suggested that students think in terms of format rather than by subject needs. Though one might deduce that it is important that libraries hold certain journal titles (as these researchers suggest), the study results also seem to indicate that teachers and librarians need to instruct students in the importance of currency of materials especially in certain subject areas, to suggest that nonprint media and journals may be equally valuable as books and to instruct students both formally and informally in the access to these materials. More needs to be done in this area before too many decisions are made on the basis of one study, especially when many other variables were not studied as possible influences, i.e., lack of knowledge on the students' part.

School/Public Library Cooperation

Since 1970 when the controversial recommendations of the Commissioner of Education of New York State were issued (stating that the elementary school library should have the responsibility to meet the library needs of all children except those in health, welfare and correctional institutions), the whole issue of specific types of cooperation between these two institutions has been discussed, researched, and debated ad infinitum. Several major studies have been completed during the 1970s providing evidence of how specific cooperation can/cannot be accomplished. These studies are found in the popular literature, and should be familiar to those working in services to children and young adults in both institutional settings. The most recent studies by Amey (1974, 1979),[54] Kitchens (1975, 1981),[55] Woolard (1977, 1980)[56] and Aaron (1977, 1978, 1980),[57] deal specifically with describing the combined school/public libraries in both the U.S. and Canada, serving as directories (Amey, Woolard), as an analysis of one successful venture (Kitchens), or as case studies (Woolard), and extensive attempts to understand why some succeed while others fail (Aaron). Certain conclusions are offered: success is more likely in communities with a small population (Woolard); one cannot expect financial savings (Woolard, Kitchens); common objectives must be present; and for success, governance and responsibility must be well established (Woolard, Kitchens). Aaron's overall conclusion is that a community able to support or now supporting separate libraries would be unlikely to succeed, but in a community with limited or unavailable services, the combined program may present a reasonable alternative. The researchers suggest that it is not a panacea, and yet there are several success stories. The specific guidelines for success seem to be based on evidence and should be taken seriously when a community contemplates the shared library.

Because attitudes and common purposes are considered so important for success, three perception studies are also valuable: Amey (1976),[58] Dyer (1976, 1977, 1978),[59] and Weech (1979, 1979).[60] Dyer's Delphi study, a large scale study assessing opinions of every group, found respondents judged cooperative efforts to be more desirable than probable due to institutional rigidity, self-preservation, and protection of territory. Dyer concluded that cooperation stands little chance of being implemented in the next fifteen years. Amey found that school and public librarians differed in their attitudes towards the concept of combined libraries. Weech found little difference in attitude between elementary and secondary school librarians, or between large or small libraries, but that school librarians were more supportive of combined facilities than public librarians. An earlier dissertation by Woolls (1973)[61] had a broader focus in terms of types of cooperative activities but was limited to Indiana school and public libraries. Again the finding that use of school libraries did not negate use of public libraries was paramount. Woolls found little cooperation including program planning, staffing, publicity, book selection, etc. A specific recommendation for interlibrary loan as a cooperating effort was made by Altman (1971, 1972)[62] in her study of title diversity and collection overlap in public secondary school libraries. Though Altman only surveyed school libraries, Tevis (1979)[63] describes the development of a cooperative program of interlibrary loan

from the public library to two public high schools through the school library. It would be interesting to check on its ongoing success. This seems to be the most natural cooperative effort, yet apparently it is an unusual case.

Programming and Services

Barass, Reitzel and Associates (1972)[64] evaluated thirty excellent public library reading and reading-related programs for preschoolers (7), elementary ages (7), young adults (6), adults (5), and multiages (5). They further selected twenty exemplary programs/services, provided description, a cost estimate, and an analysis of effectiveness (accomplished through telephone interviews to assess whether participants read more books, liked to read more, liked the library more, watched more educational TV, or did better in school). This study provides evidence to justify beginning or continuing similar programs/services. Five major types of programs emerged: preschool group activities, bookmobiles for elementary school-aged children, outreach library collections for elementary children or young adults, separate children's collections, and group activities for young adults/adults. In terms of impact, bookmobiles for children and group preschool activities ranked the highest. Other interesting results include: preschool programs had the least cost per participant; children's bookmobiles with relaxed library procedures led to a large number of participants; outreach collections involved a high cost but attracted more participants; separate children's collections were expensive in terms of per participant cost; and group activities for young adults/adults attracted the fewest regular participants but were least expensive. Some very specific findings also have implications for public libraries: those users lacking reading skills (all ages) appreciate simplified shelving; preschoolers react well to ceremony in programs (i.e., the story candle) as compared to older children and young adults who opt for informality and spontaneity; and regular schedules for outreach and bookmobile services are important as irregularities lead to attendance loss. The study provided verification that children attending public library programs do increase significantly in reading interest and the desire to learn. It also presents specific effective programs in terms of cost effectiveness and impact. The study raises fundamental questions about the appropriate roles and functions of public library systems, suggests that failure to address these questions causes less program impact but does not address the validity of objectives in judging these exemplary programs.

One example of a study evaluating creative dramatics programs as compared to storytelling to fourth and fifth graders, Ziegler (1970),[65] found that while storytelling encouraged an interest in literature and reading, creative dramatics did not.

An example of a small scale study which had important results locally, and which should be replicated in many other settings, is a study reported by Perry (1980)[66] which attempted to determine if first time users brought in by a program (in this case, summer reading programs) return and become regular library patrons. With five libraries participating in this group project, they found that of those reached for follow-up by telephone, 62 percent had returned to the public library since summer; nearly all use their school library; those coming to the public library do so mostly for use of materials, none for programs. Indirectly, other conclusions were formed including: the strong influence of parental use of public library on child use; the school library is the primary information and materials source during the school year; and children do use a traditional program such as the summer reading program and will probably continue to do so. In the summers the public library has a high priority. This study is not generalizable to other locales, but is an example of the type of study that can be completed by practitioners for local decision-making.

Services to Special Groups

Early Childhood

A pertinent review of research, as part of her doctoral dissertation, has been presented by Smardo (1978, 1980)[67] and draws from three disciplines—reading, early childhood, and library science—to examine the need for specific library services for young children. Her own study surveyed early childhood education authorities to ascertain needed areas of services, programs, materials, physical facilities, and personnel for serving children from infants to six years of age. On the basis of the literature and the survey, Smardo recommended: a focus on language arts activities, involvement of parents as active participants with their children in programs, inclusion of an educational/informational component for parents, teachers, and other child-care staff, specific programs such as "making books" (child dictating story to recorder), puppet shows and storytelling in outreach situations, programs with authors and illustrators and children, parent education courses and discussion sessions in child development, and storytelling and reading clubs which encourage parents to read selected books to children. She summarized nine specific recommendations into two common elements: the involvement of parents (and other involved adults), and an emphasis on informal prereading activities and language arts experiences (listening to stories, talking about stories, and writing about stories). On the basis of this she recommends specifically: close cooperation of public librarians with parents, teachers, and early childhood staff; and welcoming parents in short informal story/play activities with two-, three-, and four-year-old children (with parents encouraged to use followup activities).

Special Children

One area that needs study is service to exceptional children, in addition to the many special bibliographies and analyses of materials available for these special groups. As early as 1970, a demonstration/research program at the Public Library of Cincinnati and Hamilton County tried to evaluate the effectiveness of library service to exceptional children. Limper (1970)[68] described the project; but the actual research is not fully described; however, it was stated that there was statistical proof of the effectiveness of the program.

Young Adults

The young adult services area is the least researched. It is not always clear in the state-wide surveys of children's services if the young adult service area is included or excluded. In a substantial research project, Gratch reported on an indepth look at young adult users and services at the Central Public Library, Rochester, New York (1980)[69] to determine use and users, problems and needs, and how young adult information needs could best be met by the Central Library. The systematic gathering of data through interviews, needs assessments, demographic data, and a series of questionnaires of teenagers (users and nonusers) was impressive in terms of data received and the rigor in the research process.

The young adult users represented at least 12-14 percent of the total users; were predominantly secondary school students; were represented by an equal number of males and females. Slightly less than one-half were frequent users; they used the library chiefly for school-related reasons making multi-division and multi-material usage. Between one-third and one-half of all respondents had asked for assistance. Lack of consensus by the public service staff (nearly a 50/50 split) existed regarding the need to provide differential services for young adults.

Major recommendations included: need for additional staff training; need for outreach services for the alternative educational organizations and youth-related agencies; the need for a young adult librarian position at Central; for collection development and reorganization of the teen fiction; and the identification of specific goals and objectives for planning young adult services. It was suggested that there is a need for the central library to function in part similar to a school library for the students and teachers of alternate educational programs while acting differently in providing other services such as career and job information, information about recreational and leisure time activities; more activities (programs); and a printed resource directory of youth services. Because this study was of one urban public library system, results cannot be generalized, but the research instruments have been developed for replication. As well, libraries in similar communities may see similar problems and needs identified; and the major recommendations probably do apply. In a follow-up article (1981),[70] Gratch makes the point that research can lead to change, and indicates several of the study's recommendations have been or will be put into effect, including a young adult librarian position. Two earlier state-wide young adult services studies done by Joy (1968),[71] and Walton (1971)[72] had similar findings. Few libraries had separate young adult collections— when they did, there were limited funds for purchase of these materials. When there were young adult services, they were slanted to school and reference oriented needs rather than recreational. Problems identified include: lack of sufficient collections; a problem with identification of the group; a lack of contact with the schools even though more use was made by high school students of the public library reference collection than by adults. Adult cards in New Jersey at that time were given upon entrance to senior high school, making access a real issue for young adults.

The study of the historical development and philosophical basis for young adult services is described by Braverman (1974)[73] in her historical analysis of the 1920 to 1966 period of three case studies of major public library systems. Her conclusion shows a need for young adult services development today with new library services for young adults being based on a new relationship between basic philosophy, programs, and societal elements affecting youth. All of these studies show the state of young adult services today, with indications for what needs to be done to plan new services, starting with philosophical thinking, setting of objectives and priorities, and planning services based on current societal (and individual community) needs.

Professional Image of Youth Librarians

Though many role perception studies of school librarians have appeared in the literature, similar studies are not available for the children's or young adult public librarian. Three recent studies indicate new interest in this area. Calabrese (1976)[74] surveyed through a questionnaire a random sampling of children's librarians in Illinois to ascertain their perceptions of their image/status. She found a direct correlation between the librarians who were consulted on library policy matters and their feeling of increased status. Reasons given for perceiving themselves equal in status to other librarians included: better professional training, master's degree, recognition for contribution to community, recognition as a specialist in the area, and recognition of the "child" as having some importance within the library itself. Lower status feelings were due to: the "childlike" nature (telling stories, singing songs, and so forth) of the role, lower salaries and absence of administration consultation. She suggested a similar study among heads of libraries and other department heads for comparison of perceptions of the groups.

A very unusual effort to ascertain children's view of their librarians was attempted by Rogers (1978)[75] who used three methods to gain children's perceptions in one public library. A one line question resulted in some positive adjectives: 50 percent felt children's librarians were nice, and 29 percent felt they were helpful. A two page questionnaire of users did not produce useful information; however, a discussion with the "junior critics" (ages ten through fourteen) resulted in a realistic view of the role and background needed for the job. They wanted librarians to know books, like children and reading, like the work, be helpful and patient, and more specifically, to be aware of current television so they could be prepared for television tie-ins requested, and to be prepared to describe interesting and new books as well as to provide annotated booklists for older children. Rogers suggests that input from children is necessary, and that children's librarians should try techniques to elicit such response, though the task is more difficult than gathering information from adults. She recommends the Fasick and England technique as a model for obtaining user input from children.

The third study done by Kimmel (1979)[76] was to ascertain whether the librarian who exhibits more striving for professional recognition and status will have less regard for lower-class/lower-status clients. Kimmel found a significant relation between these two variables including librarians who work with adults, young adults, and children. She drew these conclusions which have implications for public library work with children: children are susceptible to being treated as lower status clients, the current move to spread staff responsibility for service and develop a "generalist" rather than an age-level specialist is difficult to reconcile with the special knowledge required of children's and young adult librarians and their willingness to serve particular groups (may cut off service to these groups); and the lack of leadership opportunities for children's librarians (road up is also road out of children's services especially when these administrative positions are cut).

CONCLUSION

After examining the conclusions of approximately 58 pertinent studies, some additional comments are appropriate. There were an even number of research studies completed between the 1970-1975, and 1976-1981 periods, approximately 29 studies during each period. Before 1975, we find a larger number of studies examining use and users, reading interests, habits, and behavior, and program evaluations. Since 1975, more studies have been state surveys, studies concerned with assessing goals and the future outlook, examining actual cooperative school/public library ventures or assessing opinions toward this issue, and assessing images of librarians working with children. There was no attempt to compare methodologies but this would be an interesting venture.

In terms of needs in the field, it would seem that we need more examination of particular services and programs especially in consideration of meeting library objectives, in meeting needs of children and young adults, and in comparison of program "effects." Basic questions on program effectiveness need to be the basis for future studies to provide information in library decision-making on programs and services. We do not need more studies looking at the combined school-public library, but we do need to have "models" for successful coordination and cooperative efforts. We need to look more indepth at which factors relate to the use of libraries by children and young adults, whether age, abilities, school curriculum, family backgrounds; we need to know more about types of media preferred and the value of different media for presenting information and literature to different age groups and to meet individual needs. The impact of professional personnel as compared to nonprofessional as children and young adult librarians on use patterns, on satisfaction of users, and on actual learning gains needs to be measured. Different patterns of display and shelving, modified access procedures, and different styles of personal and group contact with users should be compared in terms of effectiveness and user satisfaction. There is much information from research to serve as the basis for future studies; we must build on past and current research in order to test our assumptions and practices.

There are implications for decision-making in public libraries from this past research. The question is—are we reading and considering the results of pertinent research as we plan library objectives, services and programs for children and young adults?

REFERENCES

1. Gallivan, Marion F. "Research in Children's Services in Libraries; an Annotated Bibliography." *Top of the News* 30 (April 1974): 275-93.

2. Shontz, Marilyn Louise. "Selected Research Related to Children's and Young Adult Services in Public Libraries." *Top of the News* 38 (Winter 1982): 125-41.

3. Billeter, Anne. "Research and Evaluation in the Administration of Children's Work in the Public Library." *Illinois Libraries* 57 (January 1975): 10-12.

4. Kingsbury, Mary E. "Research and Children's Services of Public Libraries," in *Children's Services of Public Libraries*. Allerton Park Institute, 23d, 1977. (Urbana, Ill.: University of Illinois, 1978): 131-47.

5. Fasick, Adele M. "Research and Measurement in Library Services to Children." *Canadian Library Journal* 35 (October 1978): 341-46.

6. Lukenbill, W. Bernard. "Research in Young Adult Literature and Services" in *Libraries and Young Adults*. ed. JoAnn V. Rogers (Littleton, Colorado: Libraries Unlimited, 1979): 192-215.

7. Furman, Hazel. "Fewer Assumptions—More Research." *SLJ School library Journal* 25 (May 1979): 45.

8. Fitzgibbons, Shirley. "Research on YA Library Services' Progress." *SLJ School Library Journal* 27 (November 1980): 53.

9. Gaver, Mary. "Research on Elementary School Libraries," *ALA Bulletin* 56 (February 1962): 117-24. Also: Gaver, Mary. "Is Anyone Listening? Significant Research Studies for Practicing Librarians." *Wilson Library Bulletin* 43 (April 1969): 764-72.

10. Lowrie, Jean E. "A Review of Research in School Librarianship," in *Research Methods in Librarianship: Measurement and Evaluation*. ed. Herbert Goldhor (Urbana, Ill.: University of Illinois, Graduate School of Library Science, 1968): 51-69.

11. Aaron, Shirley Louise. "A Review of Selected Research Studies in School Librarianship, 1967-1971: Part I." *School Libraries* 21 (Summer 1972): 29-46. "Part II." *School Media Quarterly* 1 (Fall 1972): 41-48.

12. Barron, Daniel D. "Review of Selected Research in School Librarianship: 1972-1976." *School Media Quarterly* 5 (Summer 1977): 271-76 +.

13. Aaron, Shirley L. "A Review of Selected Doctoral Dissertations about School Library Media Programs and Resources, January, 1972-December, 1980." *School Library Media Quarterly* (Spring, 1982): 210-45.

14. Kingsbury, Mary. "Goals for Children's Services in Public Libraries." *SLJ School Library Journal* 24 (January 1978): 19-21.

15. Kingsbury, Mary E. "Innovations in Children's Services in Public Libraries." *Top of the News* 34 (Fall 1978): 39-42.

16. Winnick, Pauline. "Evaluation of Public Library Services to Children." *Library Trends* 22 (January 1974): 361-76.

17. Downen, Thomas W. "YA Services: 1993." *Top of the News* 35 (Summer 1979): 347-53.

18. North Carolina Central University. *A Report of the Results of a Field Survey of North Carolina Public Libraries with Regard to Their Services to Young Children.* (Durham, North Carolina Central University, 1972).

19. New York Library Association. Children's and Young Adult Services Section. Public Relations Committee. *Report.* (N.Y.: New York Library Association, 1972, mimeo).

20. *An Analytical Survey of Illinois Public Library Service to Children.* ed. Selma K. Richardson (Springfield, Ill.: Illinois State Library, 1970). Also: Richardson, Selma K. "An Analytical Survey of Illinois Public Library Services to Children: Selected Findings." *Illinois Libraries* 60 (May 1978): 497-504. Also: Fasick, Adele M. *Library Quarterly* 50 (April 1980): 266-67. (Review).

21. *A Survey of Children's Services in Ohio Public Libraries* (Columbus, Ohio: Ohio Library Association, 1979. Available $5.00, OLA, 40 S. Third St. #409, Columbus, Ohio 43215).

22. Wisconsin Department of Public Instruction. *A Report of the First Statewide Survey of Children's Services in Public Libraries of Wisconsin 1981.* (Bureau of Public and Cooperative Library Services, 1981.)

23. *Children's Services in California Public Libraries.* California Library Association and School of Library and Information Management, University of Southern California. (Research Presentation by Robert Grover and Mary Kelvin Moore. ALSC/YASD Research Forum, A.L.A. 1981 Annual Conference, San Francisco, California).

24. Hektoen, Faith H. "Researching Children's Services in Public Libraries." *SLJ School Library Journal* 26 (April 1980): 21-27. Also: Hektoen, Faith H. *The Connecticut Research Documentation Project in Children's Services.* 2 vols. (Connecticut State Library, 1981).

25. Starr, Carol and Talbot, Elizabeth. "Proposition 13: Effects on Library Services to Youth." *Top of the News* 36 (Winter 1980): 152-65.

26. Benne, Mae. *The Central Children's Library in Metropolitan Libraries* (Seattle, Wa.: University of Washington, 1978) ED 179-203. Also: Benne, Mae M. "Information Services in Central Children's Libraries." *SLJ School Library Journal* 26 (April 1980): 25.

27. Goetze, Henry J. *Reading Interests of Junior High School Students.* (Arlington, Va.: ERIC Document Reproduction Service, 1972). ED 007521.

28. Hutchinson, Margaret. "Fifty Years of Young Adult Reading: 1921-1972." *Top of the News* 30 (November 1973): 24-53.

29. Campbell, Patty; Davis, Pat; and Quinn, Jerri. "We Got There ... It Was Worth the Trip." *Top of the News* 30 (June 1974): 394-402.

30. Alm, Julie N. "Young Adult Favorites; Reading Profiles from Nine Hawaii High Schools." *Top of the News* 30 (June 1974): 403-9.

31. Wynn, Vivian and Newmark, Barbara. "Doing a Young Adult Readers' Survey: Results and Benefits:" *Top of the News* 35 (Summer 1979): 363-72.

32. "Big Change in Adolescent Reading." *Intellect* 104 (July-August 1975): 8.

33. Minudri, Regina, and Bodart, Joni. "Hip Pocket Books: the BAYA Reading Interest Report." *SLJ School Library Journal* 20 (Nov. 1973): 70-71.

34. Bodart, Joni. "The Third Time Around: BAYA Hip Pocket Reading Interest Survey III." *Top of the News* 35 (Summer 1979): 373-77.

35. Freiberger, Rema. *The New York Times Report on Teenage Reading Tastes and Habits*. (N.Y.: New York Times, 1973).

36. Stachelek, Deborah Ann. "A Comparative Study." *ALAN Newsletter* 4 (Winter 1977): unp.

37. Greenberg, Marilyn Werstein. "A Study of Reading Motivation of Twenty-three Seventh-grade Students." *Library Quarterly* 40 (July 1970): 309-17.

38. Scharf, Anne G. "Who Likes What in High School?" *Journal of Reading* 16 (May 1973): 604-7.

39. Doyen, Sally E. "A Comparison of Reading Preferences of Two Junior High Groups." *Top of the News* 36 (Winter 1980): 194-96.

40. Bard, Therese Bissen, and Leide, John E. *Reading Interests of Elementary School Children in Hawaii as Indicated by School Library Circulation Records*. (Research Presentation. ALSC/YASD Research Forum, A.L.A. 1980 Annual Conference, N.Y., N.Y.).

41. Fasick, Adele Mongan. *A Comparative Linguistic Analysis of Books and Television for Children* (Ph.D. dissertation: Case Western Reserve University, 1970).

42. Cox, Carole Alice. *Film Preference Patterns of Fourth and Fifth Grade Children*. (Ph.D. dissertation: University of Minnesota, 1975).

43. Martin, Lowell A. *Baltimore Reaches Out, Library Service to Disadvantaged*. Deiches Fund Studies of Public Library Service no. 3. (Baltimore: Enoch Pratt Free Library, 1967). Also: Martin, Lowell A. *Library Response to Urban Change: A Study of the Chicago Public Library*. (Chicago: American Library Association, 1969).

44. Martin, Lowell A. *Students and the Pratt Library: Challenge and Opportunity*. Deiches Fund Studies of Public Library Service no. 1. (Baltimore: Enoch Pratt Free Library, 1963).

45. Wilder, Philip S. *Library Usage by Students and Young Adults*. (Bloomington, Ind.: Indiana University, Graduate Library School, 1970). ED 046 472.

46. Benford, John. *Student Library Resource Requirements in Philadelphia*. (Office of Education, 1969-1971) ED 031 610, ED 031 611, Ed 057 831. Also: Benford, John. "The Philadelphia Project." *Library Journal* 96 (June 1971): 2041-47.

47. Tower, Jean D. *A Study of Changes in Children's Library Services for Selected Pittsburgh Suburbs Related to Their Population for 1960 through 1970*. (Ph.D. dissertation: University of Pittsburgh, 1972).

48. Ekechukwu, Myriette R. G. *Characteristics of Users and Non-Users of Elementary School Library Services and Public Library Services for Children*. (Ph.D. dissertation: University of Washington, 1972).

49. Fasick, Adele, and England, Claire. *Children Using Media: Reading and Viewing Preferences among the Users and Non-Users of the Regina Public Library*. (Toronto: Center for Research in Librarianship, University of Toronto, 1977).

50. Parker, Edwin B., and Paisley, William J. "Predicting Library Circulation from Community Characteristics." *Public Opinion Quarterly* 29 (Spring 1965): 39-53.

51. Moll, Joy Kaiser. *Children's Access to Information in Print: An Analysis at the Vocabulary (Reading) Levels of Subject Headings and Their Application to Children's Books*. (Ph.D. dissertation: Rutgers University, 1975).

52. Fasick, Adele M. *What Should Libraries Do For Children? Parents, Librarians, and Teachers View Materials and Services in the South Central Regional System (Ontario)*. (Hamilton, Ont.: South Central Regional Library Board, 1978). Also: Fasick, Adele M. "Parents and Teachers View Library Service to Children." *Top of the News* 35 (Spring 1979): 309-14.

53. Mancall, Jacqueline C. *Resources Used by High School Students in Preparing Independent Study Projects: A Bibliometric Approach*. (Ph.D. dissertation: Drexel University, 1978). Also: Mancall, Jacqueline C., and Drott, M. Carl. "Materials Used by High School Students in Preparing Independent Study Projects: A Bibliometric Approach." *Library Research* 1 (Fall 1979): 223-36.

54. Amey, L. J. *The Importance of Role Definition in Combining School and Public Libraries* (Arlington, Va.: ERIC Document Reproduction Service, 1974) ED 148 382. Also: Amey, L. J., ed. *The Canadian School-Housed Public Library*. (Halifax, Nova Scotia: Dalhousie University School of Library Service, 1979).

55. Kitchens, James A. *The Olney Venture: An Experiment in Coordination and Merger of School and Public Libraries.* Community Service Report no. 4. (Denton, Texas: Center for Community Services, School of Community Service, North Texas State University, 1975). Also: Kitchens, James A. *The Olney Experiment: A Venture in Coordination and Merger of School and Public Libraries.* (Denton, Texas: North Texas State University, 1981).

56. Woolard, Wilma Lee B. *The Combined School/Public Library Concept: Will It Work?* (Arlington, Va: ERIC Document Reproduction Service, 1977) ED 140 805. Also: Woolard, Wilma Lee Broughton. *Combined School/Public Libraries.* (Metuchen, New Jersey: The Scarecrow Press, Inc., 1980).

57. Aaron, Shirley L., and Smith, Sue O. *A Study of the Combined School Public Library.* (Tallahassee: State Library of Florida, 1977). ED 150 986. Also: Aaron, Shirley L. "Combined School Public Library Programs: An Abstract of a National Study." *School Media Quarterly* 7 (Fall 1978): 31-32, 49-53. Also: Aaron, Shirley. *Study of Combined School Public Libraries.* (Chicago: American Association of School Librarians, American Library Association, 1980).

58. Amey, L. J., and Smith, R. J. "Combination School and Public Libraries: An Attitudinal Study." *Canadian Library Journal* 33 (June 1976): 251-61.

59. Dyer, Esther R. "Cooperation in Library Services to Children: A Fifteen-Year Forecast of Alternatives Using the Delphi Technique." (Ph.D. dissertation: Columbia University, 1976). Also: Dyer, Esther R. "New Perspective in Cooperation in Library Service to Children." *School Media Quarterly* 5 (Summer 1977): 261-70. Also: Dyer, Esther R. *Cooperation in Library Service to Children.* (Metuchen, New Jersey: The Scarecrow Press, Inc., 1978).

60. Weech, Terry L. "Attitudes of School and Public Librarians Toward Combined Facilities." *Public Library Quarterly* 1 (Spring 1979): 51-67. Also: Weech, Terry L. "School and Public Library Cooperation—What We Should Like to Do, What We Do." *Public Libraries* 18 (Summer 1979): 33-34.

61. Woolls, E. Blanche. *Cooperative Library Services to Children in Public Libraries and Public School Systems in Selected Communities in Indiana.* (Ph.D. dissertation: Indiana University, 1973).

62. Altman, Ellen O. *The Resource Capacity of Public Secondary School Libraries to Support Interlibrary Loan: A Systems Approach to Title Diversity and Collection Overlap.* (Ph.D. dissertation: Rutgers, the State University of New Jersey, 1971). Also: Altman, Ellen O. "Implications for Title Diversity and Collection Overlap for Interlibrary Loan among Secondary Schools." *Library Quarterly* 42 (April 1972): 177-94.

63. Tevis, Ray. "Library Cooperation in Granite City: The Public Library and the High Schools, 1975-1977. *Illinois Libraries* 61 (January 1979): 6-9.

64. Barass, Reitzel and Associates, Inc. *A Study of Exemplary Public Library Reading-Related Programs for Children, Youth, and Adults.* Vols. I and II. (Cambridge, Mass.: The Associates, 1972) ED 066 197.

65. Ziegler, Elsie Mae. *A Study of the Effects of Creative Dramatics on the Progress in Use of the Library, Reading Interests, Reading Achievement, Self-Concept, Creativity, and Empathy of Fourth and Fifth Grade Children.* Ed.D. dissertation: Temple University, 1970).

66. Perry, Karen. "Research in Children's Services in Public Libraries: A Group Project in North Carolina." *Public Libraries* 19 (Summer 1980): 58-60.

67. Smardo, Frances Antoinette. *An Analytical Study of the Recommendations of Early Childhood Education Authorities with Regard to the Role of the Public Library in Serving Children from Infancy to Six Years of Age.* (Ph.D. dissertation: North Texas State University, 1978) ED 160 222. Also: Smardo, Frances A. "What Research Tells Us about Programs for Young Children." *Public Libraries* 19 (Spring 1980); 34-36.

68. Limper, Hilda K. et al. "Library Service to Exceptional Children." *Top of the News* 26 (January 1970): 193-204.

69. Gratch, Bonnie. *Central Library Young Adult Study Project.* Final Report 1978. (Research Presentation, ALSC/YASD Research Forum, A.L.A. 1980 Annual Conference, N.Y., N.Y.).

70. Gratch, Bonnie. "Research Can Lead to Change." *SLJ School Library Journal* 28 (December 1981): 35.

71. Joy, Patricia L. *Young Adults Service in Connecticut Public Libraries.* (Master's thesis: Southern Connecticut State College, 1968).

72. Walton, Jewel. "Young Adult Services in New Jersey." *New Jersey Libraries* 4 (1971): 6-12.

73. Braverman, Miriam Ruth. *Public Library and the Young Adult: The Development of the Service and Its Philosophy in the New York Public Library, Cleveland Public Library, and Enoch Pratt Free Library.* (Ph.D. dissertation: Columbia University, 1974). Also: Braverman, Miriam. *Youth, Society and the Public Library.* (Chicago: American Library Association, 1979).

74. Calabrese, Alice. "An Image/Status Study." *Illinois Libraries* 48 (December 1976): 792-94.

75. Rogers, Norma L. "The Children's Librarian as Viewed by Children" in *Children's Services of Public Libraries.* ed. Selma K. Richardson (Urbana, Ill.: University of Illinois, 1978): 57-61.

76. Kimmel, Margaret M. *Professionalization and the Orientation of Public Librarians to Lower Class Clients.* (Ph.D. dissertation, University of Pittsburgh, 1979). Also: Kimmel, Margaret M. "Who Speaks for the Children?" *SLJ School Library Journal* 26 (December 1979): 35-38.

What Works: Research about Teaching and Learning from the U.S. Department of Education

RESEARCH AND STUDY SKILLS

**Research
Finding:**

The development of student competence in research and study skills is most effective when integrated with classroom instruction through cooperative program planning and team teaching by two equal teaching partners — the classroom teacher and teacher-librarian.

Comment:

Minimal gains in research and study skills can be achieved through instruction by the classroom teacher or the teacher-librarian (TL) alone. Effective instruction depends on the cooperative effort of both teacher and TL; stated another way, scheduled library skills classes taught solely by the TL are not as effective as integrated, cooperatively planned and taught programs.

Students in flexibly scheduled schools believe that the resource center is more useful in their school work than students in scheduled schools. Flexibly scheduled resource centers provide greater academic benefits.

The TL and school resource center can have a significant effect on student achievement in information skills development and content areas when used effectively.

The use of the TL to provide spare periods or preparation time for the classroom teacher negates the possibility of a successful school program.

The term "library skills" is misleading since many of these same skills are taught by classroom teachers in various areas of the curriculum but are labelled differently (information skills; research and study skills; problem-solving skills; etc.).

Educators of TLs need to provide more leadership and instruction for TLs in cooperative program planning and teaching and in articulating and teaching research and study skills. TLs should have teaching qualifications and classroom experience prior to further training as a TL.

References:

Becker, Dale Eugene. *Social Studies Achievement of Pupils in Schools with Libraries and Schools without Libraries.* University of Pennsylvania, 1970. 172 pages. Ed.D. dissertation. (2411-A — #70-22,868)

Hodson, Yvonne D. *Values and Functions of the School Media Center as Perceived by Fourth and Sixth Graders and Their Teachers in Compared School Settings.* State University of New York at Buffalo, 1978. 188 pages. Ph.D. dissertation. (39:3-4, 1172-A — #7817042)

Smith, Jane Bandy. *An Exploratory Study of the Effectiveness of an Innovative Process Designed to Integrate Library Skills into the Curriculum.* George Peabody College for Teachers, 1978. 1974 pages. Ph.D. dissertation. (39:8, 4569 — #7902510)

Volume, issue, page and document numbers are from *Dissertation Abstracts International*. The terms teacher-librarian (TL) and resource center are used in descriptions for consistency even though they may not have been used in the original research study.

THE IMPACT OF RESOURCE CENTERS ON READING/RESEARCH SKILLS

Research Finding: **Students in schools with well-equipped resource centers and professional teacher-librarians will perform better on achievement tests for reading comprehension and basic research skills.**

Comment: There is a positive relationship between the level of resource center service available and student scholastic achievement.

In schools with good resource centers and the services of a teacher-librarian (TL), students perform significantly better on tests for basic research skills, including locational skills, outlining and notetaking and the knowledge and use of reference materials, including the use of a dictionary and encyclopedia.

In schools with good resource centers and full-time TLs, students perform significantly better in the area of reading comprehension and in their ability to express ideas effectively concerning their readings.

The greatest predictor of student achievement (of the school resource center collection size and expenditure and public library collection size and expenditure) is school resource center collection size.

Students in larger population centers and in larger secondary schools have a higher level of resource center service available to them, in terms of collection size, than students in smaller cities and in smaller schools.

References: Greve, Clyde LeRoy. *The Relationship of the Availability of Libraries to the Academic Achievement of Iowa High School Seniors.* University of Denver, 1974. 130 pages. Ph.D. dissertation. (4574-A—#75-1870)

McMillen, Ralph Donnelly. *An Analysis of Library Programs and a Determination of the Educational Justification of These Programs in Selected Elementary Schools of Ohio.* Western Reserve University, 1965. 250 pages. Ed.D. dissertation. (330-A—#66-8017)

Yarling, James Robert. *Children's Understandings and Use of Selected Library-Related Skills in Two Elementary Schools, One with and One without a Centralized Library.* Ball State University, 1968. 210 pages. Ed.D. dissertation. (3352-A—#69-4202)

COOPERATIVE PROGRAM PLANNING AND TEACHING IN SECONDARY SCHOOLS

Research Finding: **Teacher-librarians in secondary schools are not as involved in cooperative program planning and team teaching with classroom colleagues as equal teaching partners to the extent that principals, teachers and teacher-librarians themselves believe that they should be.**

Comment: If the teacher uses the resource center and consults with the teacher-librarian (TL) about planning student work, then the use of the resource center is greater. In fact, students rate schools more highly when there is agreement and communication among principal, teachers and TLs regarding program objectives and where there is planned, consistent and integrated instruction in library use. Student perceptions are valid indicators of program quality and, when carefully documented, can guide expenditures for resource center support. Districts should seek program evaluations annually from graduating students.

Important factors which affect TL involvement in curricular issues include the principal's attitude towards the TL's role, teacher preference for TLs with successful teaching experience and a teacher's frame of reference, the amount of support staff, lack of teacher understanding of the role of the TL and the potential of the resource center. The evidence is inconclusive as to the extent to which the personality of the TL makes a significant difference.

Qualified TLs rate curricular tasks as more important to their role than those without additional qualifications.

Since principals, teachers and teacher-librarians all agree on the importance of cooperative program planning and teaching, all three should be involved in resolving issues mitigating against substantial involvement. TLs need to organize more in-service training for colleagues; and educators of TLs need to revise programs to include courses which foster cooperation and understanding between teachers and TLs.

References: Corr, Graham Peter. *Factors That Affect the School Library Media Specialist's Involvement in Curriculum Planning and Implementation in Small High Schools in Oregon.* University of Oregon, 1979. 183 pages. Ph.D. dissertation. (40:6,2955–A, #7927234)

Hartley, Neil Britt Tabor. *Faculty Utilization of the High School Library.* Vanderbilt University/George Peabody College for Teachers, 1980. 199 pages. Ph.D. dissertation. (41:09, 3805, #8105512)

Scott, Marilynn Stewart. *School Library Media Center Programs: Student Perceptions as Criteria for Library Media Program Funding.* University of Southern California, 1982. Ed.D. dissertation. (43:01, 40–A, not given)

RESOURCE CENTERS AND THE CURRICULUM

Research Finding: **Secondary school resource centers are more effective when designed according to the needs of the instructional program and of the student population.**

Comment: Educational specifications developed through the cooperative efforts of teacher-librarians, teachers and administrators result in a well-planned program, and working with the architect, a physical facility designed to support this program.

Secondary school resource centers should be planned for greater flexibility. There is no optimum design for resource centers; each situation presents different problems; there are basic kinds of spaces necessary, however, regardless of the uniqueness of the school philosophy.

There has been a growing awareness of the need for instructional areas for independent study in the secondary school.

Three separate areas are required for effective programs: a general study and reading area, an animated (activity) area, and supportive work spaces for resource center staff. The general study area should constitute 50 percent of the total space, the animated areas 25-30 percent, and supportive areas 20-25 percent. The general study and reading area should be capable of seating 10 percent of the student population and additional spaces such as media and conference rooms, 5 percent of the study body. A minimum of 30 square feet per student accommodated is recommended. Space for aural and visual instructional techniques is vital.

The resource center should be located on the main floor of the building and adjacent to the majority of instructional areas but removed from areas which create excessive noise.

Greater care should be taken in planning facilities. More attention should be paid to spatial relationships. The use of color, natural and artificial lighting and architectural lines are important elements. The resource center should be equipped and furnished with those amenities which are appropriate for the physiological and psychological needs of teenagers rather than adults. This includes optimum thermal environment, furniture and color schemes.

While facilities are important, students are less concerned with the physical features of the resource center—size, location, furniture and attractiveness—than with academic relevance, accessible high quality materials and approachable and effective teacher-librarians.

References: Herald, Wayne Homer. *Planning Library Facilities for the Secondary School.* Stanford University, 1957. 178 pages. Ph.D. dissertation. (#23,174)

Kelsey, Anne Peyton. *A Study of the Criteria for the Effectiveness of Secondary School Libraries as Perceived by Selected Student Clients.* Miami University, 1976. 175 pages. Ph.D. dissertation. (4024-A–#77-1003)

Rutland, John Thomas. *A Study of the Basic Physical Facilities and Educational Roles of Secondary School Libraries.* University of Tennessee, 1971. 201 pages. Ed.D. dissertation. (#71-29,490)

Trotter, Charles Earl. *A Fortran Computer Program Designed to Identify the Physical Facilities for Public Secondary School Instructional Materials Centers.* University of Tennessee, 1964. 172 pages. Ed.D. dissertation. (#64-11,150)

PERSONALITY FACTORS IN SUCCESSFUL RESOURCE CENTERS

Research Finding: **Teacher-librarians who are less cautious and more extroverted tend to be more successful.**

Comment: Teacher-librarians tend to be responsible, emotionally stable, cautious, intellectually curious, energetic, non-assertive, and less trusting of colleagues.

TLs in exemplary resource centers are extroverted and independent; as leaders they have "tough poise."

The best set of predictors of high circulation of materials in the resource center is a high extroversion score and a high degree of curriculum involvement by the TL.

There is a significant negative correlation between cautiousness and curricular effectiveness.

High role conflict scores are significantly associated with low cautiousness, responsibility and emotional stability; high role ambiguity scores are significantly associated with low responsibility and emotional stability.

TLs differ significantly from librarians as a group as measured in 1957; they are more extroverted, demonstrate less neurotic tendency, and are more sociable.

References: Charter, Jody Beckley. *Case Studies of Six Exemplary Public High School Library Media Programs.* Florida State University, 1982. (43.02, 293-A – #DA8215239)

Hambleton, Alixe Elizabeth Lyon. *The Elementary School Librarian in Ontario: A Study of Role Perception, Role Conflict and Effectiveness.* University of Toronto, 1980. (41:06, 2338-A)

Madaus, James Richard. *Curriculum Involvement: Teaching Structures, and Personality Factors of Librarians in School Media Programs.* University of Texas, 1974. 123 pages. Ph.D. dissertation. (5436-A – #75-4965)

TEACHER-LIBRARIANS AND THE PROFESSIONAL LITERATURE

Research Finding: **Teacher-librarians need to assume more responsibility for writing about teacher-librarianship and school library programs for professional journals read by teachers and administrators.**

Comment: An accepted means of communication with teachers, that of writing in professional journals, is not being used to its fullest potential in communicating the contribution of teacher-librarians and school resource centers to education.

Articles concerning teacher-librarians tend to be accurate only when written by teacher-librarians themselves or those intimately involved with good programs. Teacher-librarians are occasionally described in disparaging terms by others.

General journals in education tend to mention teacher-librarians and media more than curriculum and association journals.

Simple identification of the resource center appears much more frequently than discussion about teacher-librarians and the resource center program.

Where articles do appear about the teacher-librarian and resource center they are more generally directed to the general aspects of teaching than to the needs of specific subject areas. The area of curricular emphasis has tended to be language arts rather than social studies, science and other core areas.

Education is emphasizing research and development but these are virtually missing in articles about library programs which appear in journals for administrators.

Acceptable levels of financing resource centers are seldom mentioned in journals aimed at school administrators. Where finances are discussed they concentrate on expensive facilities but not the ongoing expense of operation.

The cause and effect between the resources necessary for a good program and good service is omitted from journals for administrators.

Education articles in journals for administrators which mention the library program dropped from 224 in 1954-1955, to 95 in 1960 to 61 in 1969.

Information about the teacher-librarian and resource center, when included in journals for teachers and administrators, does not emphasize the curricular role of the teacher-librarian.

References: Holzberlein, Deanne Bassler. *The Contribution of School Media Programs to Elementary and Secondary Education As Portrayed in Professional Journals Available to School Administrators from 1960 to 1969.* University of Michigan, 1971. 262 pages. Ph.D. dissertation. (6466-A—#72-14,896)

Mack, Edna Ballard. *The School Library's Contribution to the Total Educational Program of the School: A Content Analysis of Selected Periodicals in the Field of Education.* University of Michigan, 1957. 389 pages. Ph.D. dissertation. (1442—LC Card No. Mic 58-1431)

Van Orden, Phyllis Jeanne. *Use of Media and the Media Center, As Reflected in Professional Journals for Elementary School Teachers.* Wayne State University, 1970. 243 pages. Ed.D. dissertation. (293-A—#71-17,324)

MEDIA DIRECTOR HAS POSITIVE EFFECT

Research Finding: **The school library media coordinator/director has a positive effect on school library program development in the school district but suffers role conflict in his/her work.**

Comment: The existence of a library media director results in significantly higher implementation of professional guiding principles for personnel, budget, purchasing, production, access and delivery systems, program evaluation, collections and facilities.

The higher the director's position is placed in the hierarchy, the wider the range of activities that can be performed in the development and regulation of school library programs and services.

The director suffers role conflict due to differences of expectations and perceptions of performance among and within principals, teacher-librarians and the supervisor of the director.

The director suffers conflict in realizing the organization's objectives due to the real, practical job world; teacher-librarians are aware of a gap between the real and ideal role behavior of the director insofar as the organization's goals are concerned, also resulting in conflict for the director.

The director finds that "the real world" makes it more difficult to attend to human needs than one ideally believes that one might be able to; teacher-librarians believe there exists a very evident gap between the real and ideal world insofar as human needs factors that they want the director to display toward them, again creating more conflict for the director.

Perception of performance is uncertain among the groups. The director works most closely with: principals, teacher-librarians and the director's supervisor.

References: *A Comparison of Perceptions and Expectations for a Central Administrative Leadership Role of Library Media Director as an Indicator of His/Her Role Behavior.* Andwood, Donald Edward. St. John's University, 1984. Ed.D. dissertations. (45/03-A. p. 693)

The Organizational Structure for State School Library Supervision and the Functions, Duties, and Activities of State School Library Supervisors. Esther Mary Carter. Ph.D. dissertation. Indiana University, 1971. (2719-A. Order No. 71-29,562)

Perceptions of "Guiding Principles" in "Media Programs: District and School." John Gordon Coleman, Jr. Ed.D. dissertation. University of Virginia, 1982. (43/07-A. p. 2206)

Role Expectations of the County School Library Supervisor and Their Perceived Fulfillment. Ruth Becker Newcombe, Ph.D. dissertation. Florida State University, 1968. (529-A. Order No. 69-11, #317)

PRINCIPAL HAS KEY ROLE

*Research
Finding:*   **The role of the principal is the key factor in the development of an effective school library program.**

Comment: The attitude of the principal to the role of the teacher-librarian (TL) affects the TL's involvement in curricular issues.

Exemplary school library resource centers are characterized by strong administrative support.

Principals in schools with exemplary resource center programs establish evaluation procedures, integrate the resource center in instructional programs, encourage student and teacher use and provide flexible scheduling.

TLs continue to view the support of the principal as critical to program improvement.

Principals may serve as a barrier to the improvement of resource center programs if they do not perceive the need for change and do not have the necessary expertise on which to base improvement decisions.

References: Anderson, Edward Lawrence. *The Educational Media Building Coordinator: His Role as Perceived by School Administrators.* Michigan State University, 1970. 163 pages. Ph.D. dissertation. (4374-A, #71-2019)

Charter, Jody Beckley. *Case Study Profiles of Six Exemplary Public High School Library Media Programs.* Florida State University, 1982. 321 pages. Ph.D. dissertation. (43:2, 293-A, #DA 8215239)

Corr, Graham Peter. *Factors that Affect the School Library Media Specialist's Involvement in Curriculum Planning and Implementation in Small High Schools in Oregon.* University of Oregon, 1979. 183 pages. Ph.D. dissertation. (40:6, 2955-A, #7927234)

Guise, Benjamin R. *A Survey of Public School Library Resources in Arkansas.* North Texas State University, 1972. 152 pages. Ed.D. dissertation. (33:4, 4444-A #73-2904)

Hellene, Dorothy Lorraine Ingalls. *The Relationships of the Behaviors of Principals in the State of Washington to the Development of School Library Media Programs.* University of Washington, 1973. 161 pages. Ed.D. dissertation. (3835-A)

Shields, Dorothy McDonald. *A Fault Tree Approach to Analyzing School Library Media Services.* Brigham Young University, 1977. 203 pages. Ed.D. dissertation. (2392-A, #77-23,174)

Walker, Carol Chism. *The Role of the Principal in the Provision of Effective Library Services in Selected Indiana Elementary Schools.* Indiana University, 1982. 107 pages. Ed.D. dissertation. (42:11, 4683-A, #DA 8209883)

LIBRARIES COMPLEMENT RESOURCE CENTERS

*Research
Finding:*   **Students generally use libraries as a complement to school resource centers and prefer books to other resources.**

Comment: TLs believe that students are more aware of resources and services than they really are.

Only a small percentage of students use the resource center regularly and these tend to be better students.

In order of frequency, students use books (through the card catalog) as the medium of choice, periodicals (through the *Readers' Guide*) second and encyclopedias third. Periodicals used tend to be in the resource center.

Students have a more positive attitude to the resource center when there is a full-time TL.

Most students use the public and/or college library as a complement to the school resource center.

References: Ducat, Mary Peter Claver. *Student and Faculty Use of the Library in Three Secondary Schools.* Columbia University, 1960. 302 pages. DLS dissertation. (LC Card No. Mic 60-2449)

Durand, Joyce Jenkins. *A Bibliometric Study of Student Use of Periodicals for Independent Research Projects in High School Libraries with Implications for Resource Sharing.* Georgia State University, 1985. 140 pages. Ph.D. dissertation. (46/08-A, 2115)

Geppert, Alida L. *Student Accessibility to School Library Media Center Resources as Viewed by Media Specialists and Compared to Students in Southwestern Michigan Secondary Schools.* Western Michigan University, 1975. 134 pages. Ed.D. dissertation. (#76-8463)

Stroud, Janet Gossard. *Evaluation of Media Center Services by Media Staff, Teachers, and Students in Indiana Middle and Junior High Schools.* Purdue University, 1976. 186 pages. Ph.D. dissertation. (37/08-A, 4674, #77-1783)

MORE CONTINUING EDUCATION NEEDED

Research Finding:
More and more varied continuing education opportunities need to be provided for teacher-librarians in order for them to pursue their own professional growth.

Comment:
Teacher-librarians respond more to professional development opportunities which are of high quality and which offer new and creative ideas applicable to the job site.

Time, location and inferior quality detract TLs from attending professional development programs.

Programs should be offered by school districts on serving specific client groups, such as special education teachers and students.

University continuing education programs should reflect the expressed needs of TLs, such as microcomputer applications to their role and the resource center.

Workshops presented at conferences can provide effective continuing education by effecting changes in knowledge and attitudes toward a particular topic.

Continuing education opportunities need to be provided in a variety of formats and approaches.

References:
Bell, Geraldine Watts. *Determining a Job Performance Basis for the Development of an Individualized Staff Development Program for School Library Media Specialists.* University of Alabama, 1977. 183 pages. Ed.D. dissertation. (DA 39:3-4, 1904-A)

Buckley, Cozetta White. *Media Services for Exceptional Students: An Exploratory Study of the Practices and Perceptions of Library Media Specialists in Selected Southern States.* University of Michigan, 1978. 239 pages. Ph.D. dissertation. (5781-A)

Cantor, Phyllis Fine. *Role Expectations for Library Media Services Held by Library Media Specialists, School Administrators, and Teachers.* Columbia University, 1975. 211 pages. DLS dissertation. (#76-12,728)

Davie, Judith Fields. *A Survey of School Library Media Resources for Exceptional Students in Florida Public Schools.* Florida State University, 1979. 220 pages. Ph.D. dissertation. (Volume 40, Number 09, 4786-A)

Hawley, Catherine Agnes. *An Examination of Management/Communication Perceptions of Library Media Managers.* University of Colorado, 1982. Ph.D. dissertation. (Volume 43, Number 04, 962-A)

Schlieve, Paul Lynn. *Perceived Microcomputer Professional Development Needs of Wisconsin Public School Library/Media Specialists.* Southern Illinois University, 1981. 146 pages. Ph.D. dissertation. (Volume 42, Number 10, 4413-A)

Stone, Elizabeth W. *A Study of Some Factors Related to the Professional Development of Librarians.* The American University, 1968. Ph.D. dissertation. (Volume 29, Number 04, 1240-A)

Tassia, Margaret Rose. *Conference Programs as a Vehicle for Continuing Education: A Case Study of an Educational Gains Workshop Presented to School Library Media Specialists.* University of Pittsburgh, 1978. 214 pages. Ph.D. dissertation. (Volume 40, Number 02, 514-A).

The Importance of School Libraries/Resource Centres and Teacher-Librarians in British Columbia Schools

The British Columbia Library Association

INTRODUCTION

In the fall of 1982 a number of changes were made in the educational finance provisions of the province of British Columbia. Severe cutbacks placed school resource centres and teacher-librarians in jeopardy but the solidarity of teachers, including teacher-librarians, prevented special representations on behalf of particular interest groups. The British Columbia Library Association (BCLA), on the other hand, was a group outside the B.C. Teachers' Federation (BCTF) but vitally concerned with school library services. Through ongoing liaison activities, the BCLA prepared the following brief and presented it in person to school boards at public meetings at the request of local chapters of the British Columbia School Librarians' Association, a separate professional body affiliated with the BCTF. This type of advocacy and cooperation is essential to effective liaison and stronger foundations for school libraary service.

WHY SCHOOL LIBRARIES ARE IMPORTANT

The school library/resource centre is an integral part of education at all levels. It is just one of the links in the total library educational service spectrum in which there exists university, college, and public libraries each providing a specified level of service.

A school library exists specifically to support, enrich, and implement the curriculum taught in a specific school and no other library can substitute adequately for that school library. Public libraries do not buy curriculum-related materials; they serve the more general information and recreational needs of the public at all ages and educational backgrounds in society, and do not have the financial resources to expand that mandate. The materials purchased by college and university libraries are of an advanced nature in support of college and university level curricula. Each type of library cooperates and shares materials and information where possible through various mechanisms ranging from formal networks to consultation, to extend the use and value of expenditures, to ensure the best possible service is given to the public at the least amount of cost.

The school library is more than just a repository for books and other media. It is a place where services emanate and flow:

To Students: to spark interest, to develop keen understandings, to learn research skills necessary to deal with the more complex research methods and resources for higher learning, and a place to work and grow.

To Teachers: a valuable resource to assist them in their goal of developing informed adults who will be capable not only of existing in society, but capable of making decisions and discoveries to contribute to and enrich society.

Today there is renewed emphasis on the need to arouse intellectual curiosity, to encourage research, to help the exceptional or gifted, to understand and help the socially and culturally deprived, and to stimulate understanding and use of basic skills. The library is unique in that it gives service to all school people from the kindergarten child to administrator and to those with special needs at all levels of ability. The school library/resource centre is STRATEGIC in providing the SETTING (the library/resource centre), the TOOLS (books, magazines, films, recordings, computers, displays), and the GUIDANCE (the teacher-librarian working cooperatively with the teacher) to nurture their goals.

THE SCHOOL LIBRARY AS AN AGENCY FOR SOCIALIZATION

By fostering and challenging students to seek and develop interests, to search out information and to think, the school library does much more than develop thinkers and doers. It assists in the child's socialization process in relation to others and in developing a better understanding of life. It helps to develop good citizens. Research has even shown that the presence of a school library is a factor in reducing delinquency and crime in society.[1]

SCHOOL LIBRARIES FOSTER INDEPENDENT THINKING AND LEARNING

It is becoming increasingly important for students to learn to function well in an information society. In order to do this, they must develop both general information searching skills and more specific knowledge of community and national resources. School libraries are vital in training pupils to *effectively* utilize research methods and resources—important skills both for students continuing their education beyond the secondary level and for those entering the job market. The ability to carry out an inquiry independently is an essential lifetime skill for everyone. A study of urban school libraries demonstrated that elementary schools with good librarians provide a quantity and variety of reference skill learning experiences far superior to that acquired in schools without professionally staffed libraries.[2]

ROLE OF THE TEACHER-LIBRARIAN

A teacher-librarian is a highly-skilled professional with specialized competencies in school librarianship and media services. Teacher-librarians are involved in curriculum development and in cooperative teaching situations where their instructional responsibility is based on their subject expertise. As specialists in the selection, organization, management, and the utilization of all book and nonbook media, the teacher-librarian is concerned with the quality of use of reference materials, research skills, and learning materials. The teacher-librarian is involved in pre-planning before a unit of study begins and ensures that appropriate materials are available. Teacher-librarians not only assume an active role in curriculum planning but also in strategies for implementation and evaluation. Research has indicated that with the presence of the teacher-librarian on the school staff and the extent to which individualized instruction is implemented by the school library, that recommended academic standards significantly rise with the presence of an adequately funded and staffed school resource centre.[3]

The role of the school library, as indeed of any library, is not a storehouse for books and other materials, but a place where people go for informational and learning purposes. The teacher-librarian promotes literacy and provides an environment that encourages students to study and learn. The needs of the school curriculum are supported in the library and to encourage greater literacy, reading habits are stimulated by books and the imaginative qualities of the teachers and teacher-librarian. Research shows that there is a strong relationship between teacher-librarians' interaction and overall student use of the library. There is documentation showing that schools having high overall library use are those with active teacher-librarians.[4]

SCHOOL LIBRARIES INCREASE ACADEMIC ACHIEVEMENT

Many studies show that a professionally staffed, well-stocked school library makes a significant difference in the level of academic achievement of students. One study demonstrates that good school libraries strongly increase the academic motivation of pupils.[5] In another study, nine different standardized tests were used to examine the academic achievement of high school seniors in 232 schools. Good library facilities and service were found to have a significant effect on students' scholastic successes.[6] A further study of 121 schools found that reading comprehension, and knowledge and use of reference materials were superior in the schools with good libraries and full-time teacher-librarians.[7] Yet another research report indicates that the number of library books per student positively affects achievement test scores in reading and mathematics.[8]

CONCLUSION

"Public education in the Province of British Columbia is established with the philosophy that every child in the Province will have the opportunity to develop to the fullest potential not only as an individual but also as a member of society."[9]

The school library/resource centre needs the moral and material support of the Board to effectively carry out this aim and to assist students to become informed decision makers and life-long learners.

(Adopted by the British Columbia Library Association Executive Board, December 4, 1982.)

FOOTNOTES

1. "Brief to the New Zealand Advisory Committee on Youth and Law," *NZLA Library Life*, (February 1, 1982), reprinted in *Feliciter*, 28:10 (October, 1982), p. 9.

2. Willson, Ella, "Evaluating Urban Centralized Elementary School Libraries," Wayne State University, Ed.D., 1965.

3. Aaron, Shirley, "The Instructional Role of the School Library Media Specialist: What Research Says to Us Now," *School Media Quarterly*, 9:4 (Summer 1981), pp. 281-85.

4. Mancall, Jacqueline C., and M. Carl Drott, "Tomorrow's Scholars: Patterns of Facilities Use," *School Library Journal*, 26:7 (March, 1980), pp. 99-103.

5. "The Effect of Commonwealth Libraries upon Academic Motivation," *The Australian Journal of Education*, 18:2 (June, 1974), pp. 113-23.

6. Greve, Clyde L., "The Relationship of the Availability of Libraries to the Academic Achievement of Iowa High School Seniors," University of Denver, Ph.D., 1974.

7. McMillan, Ralph D., "An Analysis of Library Programs and a Determination of the Educational Justification of These Programs in Selected Elementary Schools of Ohio," Western Reserve University, Ed.D., 1965.

8. Saterfiel, Thomas H., "The Relationship between Student Achievement and Accreditation Variables Associated with the Student's School," ERIC Document 157913, 1974.

9. British Columbia Ministry of Education Administrative Bulletin for Secondary Schools (1974); Ministry of Education Administrative Bulletin for Elementary Schools (1971).

GENERAL REFERENCES

Barron, Daniel. "A Review of Selected Research in School Librarianship: 1972-1976," *School Media Quarterly*, 5:1 (Fall, 1976), pp. 271-89.

Lowrie, Jean Elizabeth. *Elementary School Libraries*. 2d ed. Metuchen, New Jersey. Scarecrow, 1970.

Sources and Resources: A Handbook for Teacher-Librarians in British Columbia. Victoria, Ministry of Education, 1978.

Part 2
THE COMMITMENT

Being a teacher-librarian carries with it a commitment, a professional obligation or pledge, to act as an advocate for school library program development and the need for effective teacher-librarians. The teacher-librarian actively supports the cause and exercises that personal ability and power which grants professionals the capacity to do something. Too often we feel that we don't have power in the sense of total control over our destinies but we do have the ability to exercise influence and provide leadership. We also have control over our commitment to develop and maintain a favorable image and goodwill.

Program advocacy is the missing link in our professional preparation and role definition. If we don't stand up and speak for ourselves certainly no one else is going to. As Jim Bowman points out, it is never school libraries which are endangered, but teacher-librarians themselves. Where do you stand?

PERSISTENCE

Nothing in the world can take
the place of **PERSISTENCE** . . .

Talent will not;
    Nothing is more common than
    Unsuccessful men and women
    with talent . . .

Genius will not;
    Unrewarded genius is
    Almost a proverb . . .

Education will not;
    The world is full
    Of educated derelicts . . .

PERSISTENCE and **DETERMINATION**
    Alone are omnipotent . . .

The slogan "**PRESS ON**" has solved,
    And always will solve,
    The problems of the human race

— *Anonymous*

EMERGENCY LIBRARIAN 12:5

Program Advocacy: The Missing Element

Ken Haycock

There is ample evidence in both education and librarianship that few members of the public are aware of the nature and scope of library service for young people and that few administrators are aware of the potential of quality programming for this group of users. Regrettably, while one might charge librarians with responsibility for this situation, it is only these same librarians who can bring about needed change. Collectively, it is still possible to develop support for programs, services and growth but it is individuals who have to articulate the value of the program, provide visible evidence of use and prove the essential nature of the service. The day has passed when system-level advocates can protect and promote services and positions on their own. The scrutiny of expenditure includes the individual school and the individual library. Are we prepared for this challenge or are we perhaps too complacent, too conservative, too timid ... even too uncommitted? Clearly, a more positive and professional approach than talking only to each other and belabouring the problems of the ages is needed in order to gain support for the maintenance and extension of services and programs.

A key element in any strategy for change is effective program advocacy with a vigorous public relations program. This advocacy is based on a systems approach to development: planning, research, examining alternatives, formulating strategy, monitoring, modification, evaluation. Time and financial resources must be allocated to public relations activities, and this is not just advertising or promotion for these are only two of the tools needed to develop an informed network of support within the institution and the community. Public relations starts with planning and fact finding; it emphasizes effective communication when and where it counts and requires objective evaluation. Most important, public relations, like any emerging service priority, begins with an attitude of self-analysis. Why are we involved in education and/or librarianship to start with? How committed are we to library service to youth? How convinced are we of the need to "market the product?"

A program of action requires a solid philosophical foundation to be successful. It also requires the self-confidence necessary to speak well for youth and the skills essential for good communication. Do we have a clear, logical response for the administrator or trustee who questions the value of storytelling, story reading or puppetry? Do we leave the impression that these are simply traditional programs or entertainment or can we articulate their important contributions to creativity, language acquisition and reading readiness, when planned and implemented with professional expertise? Do we have a clear and logical response when queried about the value of outreach for young teenagers by the administrator or trustee who forgets that library use drops dramatically at age twelve, during the critical years in the development of lifelong readers?

What are the system's written goals of library service for young people? What are the objectives for this year? Are they recorded anywhere? Are they specific and manageable? What are the major strengths and weaknesses of our program? What should be changed and improved? What can be improved most easily?

It is important to identify the specific audiences that we are trying to reach and the best approaches to addressing them. Surely we would promote our services differently with each of a group of young adults, a group of librarians, the system's administrators, and a community organization. Who is it that we're trying to reach in the branch, the school, the district, the community? What approaches are we using? Which have been most successful with each group? With this background information alternatives in a concerted public relations program can be carefully planned and well implemented.

Granted, special skills need to be developed. Why don't our systems conduct sophisticated training sessions for staffs on leading workshops with community and professional groups, public speaking, the wide variety of methods for promoting programs and how to develop political awareness?

It is almost axiomatic that librarians need to become politicized for this is the era of special interest groups and lobbies. The library voice for the needs of young people must not be muted. When did you last attend a meeting of your board? Do you ensure through your associations that these public meetings are held in the evening when members of the public and staff can attend? In my experience as a library trustee members of staff rarely attend meetings, few members of staff ever introduce themselves to trustees, and no member or staff ever button-holes trustees to provide them with useful information or to elicit support. Has your group considered dividing responsibilities for improving the knowledge and support of individual trustees and administrators? Have you recognized what some call a "legislative liaison" obligation? Have you established an influential advisory committee (a "friends" group) on service for young people? Have you encouraged the appointment of a young adult to the public library board? Have you asked elected trustees at open meetings what they will do to improve library service for young people? Without regard to the myriad of labour concerns, have you involved adult volunteers in your programs? Schools and libraries know that these individuals can be their best ambassadors in the community. These and similar techniques cannot fail to encourage continuing support for youth and to assure that this service holds a rightful place in the library list of priorities.

Program advocacy is for believers. It requires commitment and dedication to the continuation of the service as well as to the best performance tomorrow on the job. It also requires an objective recognition of the essence of power and how it pervades the work place. Service does not sell itself; librarians must inform decision-makers of the value of their service and the need for adequate funding. Bridges should be built for support before it is crucial and then used again and again in an informed and supportive communication network.

Start with small groups and build influential contacts. If we really believe in the product then we must get out and sell it! It is crucial that we be articulate and assertive. If we don't speak for the best library services for the young, no one will.

Who Speaks for Us?
Power, Advocacy and the Teacher-Librarian

Gene Burdenuk

Simply stated, teacher-librarians in the province of Ontario *had* power but no longer do. At the same time, school librarianship in Ontario is suffering from a crisis of complacency and credibility.

Consider these:

- In 1967 there were 21 full time individuals with library/media responsibilities employed by the Ministry of Education. In 1984 there is not one individual remaining with full time responsibility for school libraries

- In 1974 there were 6 full time faculty members involved in education for school librarianship at four Faculties of Education in Ontario. In 1984 there will not be one full time person involved in education for school librarianship

- Both accredited graduate library schools (University of Toronto and University of Western Ontario) have cut back on their school librarianship related graduate courses with the University of Toronto Faculty of Library and Information Science suspending its program for the next three years

- In 1984 we have fewer teacher-librarians in Ontario, fewer library consultants and fewer school libraries than we had in 1974

- In 1984 we are spending less money on learning materials than we did in 1974

- The Ontario School Library Association has difficulty in getting people to run for executive positions in the organization

"Who speaks for us?" By now the answer should be evident — no one speaks for us — we must speak for ourselves!

- Now is the time to stand up and be counted!

- Now is the time to say "I'm mad as hell and won't take it anymore!"

- Now is the time to begin working with your feet and not your seat!

- Now is the time to speak up or forever hold your peace!

You and you alone have the responsibility for:

- articulating the value of resource based programs

- providing evidence that it works

- proving that it is essential and integral to the learning process

Lorne MacRae, director, media services group, Calgary Board of Education, writing in *Emergency Librarian* quotes Pogo in describing the plight of Canadian school librarianship: "we have found the enemy and he is us." He continues by saying, "Not only must we save our seals and whales and Siberian tigers, and silver darters, we must also save our school librarians."[8] Ken Haycock questions whether teacher-librarians "are too complacent, too conservative, too timid ... and even too uncommitted?" "Clearly," he continues, "a more positive and professional approach than talking only to each other and belabouring the problems of the ages is needed in order to gain support for the maintenance and extension of services and programmes."[6] What both are talking about is an increased advocacy role for the teacher-librarian.

Joyce Birch defines advocacy as "an attempt to favourably influence the attitudes of a designated group or individual. An advocate is someone with a cause to promote."[1] Some teacher-librarians question the need for, and the ethics of, embarking on an advocacy campaign. And yet important documents such as Ontario's *Partners in Action* clearly identify one of the six major roles of the teacher-librarian as program advocacy.

> "It is important for the teacher-librarian to articulate clearly the unique contribution that he or she can make to the learning activities of the school. Time must be set aside on a regular basis to communicate with the principal and to discuss issues in a logical, professional manner. Similarly, classroom teachers need to be made aware of the unique contribution of the teacher-librarian and at the same time helped to realize how important it is that the teacher's special knowledge of individual students, of appropriate teaching techniques and of subject content be included in any planning sessions on student use of library resource centres and library materials."9:38

If there is a failure in school librarianship over the last 20 years it has been the lack of effort, emphasis, and focus placed on the role of the teacher-librarian as advocate. What is needed now is an advocacy campaign to bring attention to the importance of school libraries to the education of the child.

When embarking on an advocacy campaign it might be helpful to develop a systematic process in order to achieve the desired results. The first step is to determine aims and objectives. These aims and objectives might be gleaned from a needs assessment which could involve a survey of the staff, students and possibly parents. They might evolve through intuition, but be careful here, because frequently how you perceive your school library program is not the way others do so. Your aims and objectives should be specific and measurable so that when your campaign is over some assessment of its success can be made. Typical objectives might be to clarify the role of the teacher-librarian with staff members, to establish and maintain a school library advisory committee, and to work with the principal and staff in developing priorities for the school library program.

The next step in the process involves identifying the audience. There is a tendency when organizing public relations campaigns to focus on the users or the already committed. Dispalys, as attractive as they may be, do little good if not seen by the non-user groups. Similarly campaigns aimed at the school level will not heighten awareness of the successes of the library program within the community or with school board administration. It is important to identify all of the various audiences that can have an impact on school library programs. These include the administration of the school, teachers, students, board administrators, the community and school trustees.

After having identified your audience you must determine the characteristics of the group. This will help in developing appropriate strategies that may be used. What are the interests, likes and dislikes of your audience? What works and what doesn't work with them? A long 20-minute slide/tape presentation may work well with a local parents group but may bore a group of time-pressed principals. A campaign aimed at the community will take a different approach in communities where the majority do not have children in the public schools

than one in which school-aged children predominate. Advocacy campaigns aimed at principals will vary according to the perceived leadership style of the principal concerned. Just as a school library program is unique to a school, so too is the advocacy campaign. What is important, however, is that a clear and comprehensive profile of the audience be undertaken before the campaign is launched.

The next step in the process entails determining strategies. These strategies will be dependent upon the aims and objectives, the location, the group size, the financial resources and the time available. A presentation to a group of trustees or senior board administrators may require more preparation, thought and polish than perhaps a presentation to a school staff. Cracking a new department or a new principal might be more delicate than working with an already committed principal or department head. There should be some expectation that the degree of effort put into the campaign leads to a comparable degree of success.

Selecting a means of communication is the next important step in the process. Once again an awareness of the aims of the program, the intended audience, and the characteristics of the audience will assist in selecting the most appropriate medium. Consideration should be given to using the newspaper, newsletters, local cable companies, radio, television, and the host of other communication media. The important thing is to make the most effective use of the media that is available and to ensure that the message that is being intended is being transmitted.

The last three steps in the process involve Implementing, Evaluating, and Redesigning, reinforcing the fact that the end of one advocacy campaign is the beginning for the next. As Joyce Birch so aptly states, "Like a summer sun tan the shining image created by one effective public relations campaign soon fades unless it is part of a long term continuous programme."1

Examples of concerted, comprehensive and systematic advocacy campaigns can be found throughout Canada. Perhaps the best example of effective advocacy has taken place in Manitoba under the direction of the Manitoba School Library Audio Visual Association (MSLAVA). Over the last several years MSLAVA has been involved in the annual School Library Event (SLE). SLE has had as its objectives:

1. To encourage effective use of existing library resources and services over the entire school year.

2. To publicize the components and dimensions of a school library program.

3. To increase awareness of the role and function of the teacher-librarian.

The campaign included sending out kits containing suggestions for activities to help teacher-librarians in Manitoba to meet these objectives. Also involved were two library-related province-wide contests. SLE contains a number of monthly kits with objectives and strategies for several activities ranging from clarifying the role of the school librarian with staff members to developing public relations with parents, taxpayers, trustees and superintendents. The impact of MSLAVA's SLE culminated in the proclamation by the Minister of Education of *Manitoba School Library Week*.

MSLAVA is not comprised of a large group of librarians. They have, however, been successful in furthering the state of school libraries in Manitoba through an effective, systematic and comprehensive advocacy program. They serve as an example of what can be accomplished through increased advocacy.

POWER AND THE TEACHER-LIBRARIAN

Closely related to the concept of advocacy is the concept of power. While advocacy has been defined as "an attempt to favourably influence the attitudes of a designated group or individual" power can be defined as the ability "to affect the course of action of an enterprise to a greater degree than others" or to "influence other decisions." Power is not the same as authority, as authority is the right to act or to require others to act on behalf of the organization's purposes. In a school setting only the principal has authority. Often those with little authority exert considerable influence or power on the decision making process. We all know, for example, members of the school staff who are not in a position of authority and yet wield tremendous influence. Teacher-librarians as a group have no authority but they can have power.

An exhaustive search of the literature was undertaken to locate any articles on the concept of power or influence and the school librarian. Only a handful of articles turned up with only one being directly related.[2] In order to find more information on the concept of power in the school setting the search was extended to include teacher power in the school. Once again very few articles were discovered. One article, "Becoming Influential with Administrators"[10] does, however, provide a model for home economists and family studies teachers but which could be adapted for teacher-librarians as follows.

STEPS TO BECOMING INFLUENTIAL WITH ADMINISTRATORS

Changing Ourselves

Teacher-librarians must stop blaming others for not understanding the role of the library in the school. They must also stop believing that eventually good will triumph and everyone on the school staff will see the light and come to believe in the importance of the library in the educational process. Teacher-librarians must also take the responsibility for the lack of influence and status that school libraries have at the local, provincial and national levels. Teacher-librarians have not clearly articulated the importance of school libraries in the educational process nor of the role that they perform as part of this process.

Developing a Clearer Role Definition

Research has shown that teacher-librarians themselves are not clear about their role. As recently as 1981, teacher-librarians still consistently placed higher value on the librarianship aspects of their job than on the cooperative program planning and teaching functions.[11] The perceptions of our role in the school is based on how students, teachers, and principals observe us performing our role. A continuing emphasis on the performance of library-related functions denigrates our position as a teaching partner and as an integral member of the staff. Furthermore, if we do not have a clear perception of what our role is, how can we expect others to understand our position?

Defining your role could begin by asking a number of questions. These might include:

- How much time do you spend on the various aspects of the school library?

- How hard have you tried to develop cooperative, resource-based programs in your school?

- What are the strengths and weaknesses of your program?

- How can you do better?

- What are your long range plans?

- What would happen to the school if the library closed tomorrow?

Remember too that defining your role serves no purpose unless that role is clearly communicated to the members of the staff.

Working with Your Feet—Not Your Seat

Teacher-librarians as a group have been shown to be dedicated, hard working and extremely creative. But they also have been found to be overly cautious. "This cautiousness prevents librarians from implementing some of their creative and innovative ideas and may in part explain why librarians tend to perform most often, those tasks that relate to library expertise rather than those which involve the librarian in the teaching program."[5] Working with your feet entails:

1. attending meetings and speaking up.

2. writing letters and speaking out.

3. volunteering for school activities.

4. running for association or federation offices.

5. becoming a spokesperson on important issues.

Gaining Power by Establishing a Community Power Base

School boards, superintendents, directors of education and principals all listen and respond to community pressure. Librarians can be proactive in the community and seek community support for school library initiatives. It is very important that the public understands the need for school libraries in the educational system. Once that understanding has been attained the school library will be on a firm foundation and less likely to be attacked or restrained. Some suggestions here:

1. Establish a community school library advisory committee.

2. Run promotions on cable television.

3. Organize public forums.

4. Get actively involved in community service groups.

5. Send a regular newsletter home to parents.

6. Establish links with other information agencies in the community.

7. Arrange for presentations to the board administration or trustees.

8. Develop an advocacy campaign as described earlier in this paper.

Remember that no teacher-librarian is an island, entire of itself. The establishment of a community power base will lead to a greater community awareness of the role of the school library, greater community pride and by extension, greater administrative pride for the library.

Gaining Power by Developing a Professional Power Base

The success and reputation of many of the leaders in the field of school librarianship and indeed, education as a whole, is frequently related to their active involvement in professional associations. This involvement brings with it new contacts with new people with new ideas. It is this involvement that provides you with confidence and renewed strength for your own ideas. Teacher-librarians have not, in the past, been actively involved in a leadership role in professional teacher association activity. As a result, when decisions are made, they are frequently made without teacher-librarian input.

1. Get active in your school staff association.

2. Get active at the district level.

3. Get involved with your provincial school library subject council.

4. Get involved with the Canadian School Library Association.

5. Just get involved.

Gaining Power by Developing an Expertise Power Base

French and Bacon[4] have been widely cited in the literature of educational administration for providing one of the most important models for understanding the bases of social power. They have identified five sources of power in an organization: reward power, coercive power, legitimate power, referent power and expert power. Additional research has shown that in a school setting only the last three sources normally are perceived to be operative. Teacher-librarians do not have legitimate power as the principal is the only person delegated with this authority. Teacher-librarians can develop referent power by engaging in the kinds of activities cited above.

The other major way of developing a power base is through expertise. There has been a significant shift in the power base of many schools over the last few years as educational trends change. When special education was the focus those with special education expertise exercised a certain degree of power. As computers began to be introduced into our schools a new power base was established with those who had computer expertise. Teacher-librarians can gain access to this power by developing expertise in appropriate areas:

1. Take additional courses in the special education, gifted, reading and computer areas.

2. Enroll in Master of Library Science courses.

3. Pursue Master of Education programs.

CONCLUSION

We are in the information age and our function is working with information. As Lancaster stated:

> Libraries, as we know them now, have a limited life expectancy. In the long term, they will become museums or archives, repositories of the records of the past, serving warehouse and delivery functions but offering little service.... The librarian, as a skilled information professional will have a much longer lived function.... The future of the librarian depends on his ability and willingness to move out of the library.[7:169]

Are you prepared to meet the challenge?

BIBLIOGRAPHY

1. Birch, Joyce. "Advocacy: What Is It?" *MSLAVA Journal*, Volume 9, Number 1 (October, 1981), pp. 4-7.

2. Bowman, Jim. "Power and the School Librarian—Starting Here, Starting Now." *Emergency Librarian*, Volume 9, Number 1 (September-October, 1981), pp. 6-11.

3. Burdenuk, Eugene. "The Rose Report and School Librarianship in Ontario." *Focus,* Volume 9, Number 2 (April, 1983), pp. 11-12.

4. French, Jr., John R. and Bertram Raven. "The Bases of Social Power." In *Group Dynamics: Research and Theory*, edited by D. Cartwright and A. F. Zander. 3rd edition. New York: Harper and Row, 1968.

5. Hambleton, Alixe. "Static in the Educational Intercom: Conflict and the School Librarian." *Emergency Librarian*, Volume 6, Number 5-6 (May-August, 1979), pp. 5-7.

6. Haycock, Ken. "Program Advocacy: The Missing Element." *Emergency Librarian*, Volume 7, Number 4-5 (March-June, 1980), p. 3.

7. Lancaster, F. W. *Libraries and Librarians in an Age of Electronics.* Information Resources Press, 1982.

8. MacRae, Lorne. "Too Many Chickens ... Too Few Hogs." *Emergency Librarian*, Volume 6, Number 5-6 (May-August, 1979), pp. 8-9.

9. Ontario Ministry of Education. *Partners in Action: The Library Resource Centre in the School Curriculum.* Toronto, 1982.

10. Simerly, Coby Bunch. "Becoming Influential with Administrators." *Illinois Teacher*, September/October, 1977, pp. 23-26.

11. Staple, E. Susan. "60 Competency Ratings for School Media Specialists." *Instructional Innovator*, November, 1981, pp. 19-23.

Power and the School Librarian—Starting Here, Starting Now

Jim Bowman

To examine power and the role of school librarians it is necessary to look first at power in general terms as it applies to school libraries, and then to analyse the power structure of the school system and where teacher-librarians fit into it. It then becomes critical to look at education today and at the forces affecting schools and perhaps the survival of teacher-librarians.

"Politics" has unfortunately become a four-letter word used in a negative sense, such as 'keep politics out of this.' And terms such as "democracy" or "he's got principles, he's not a politician" are bandied about like holy writ. Well, people who do that have got it all backwards. It's politics that has created the pretty fair conditions in which we live. Those in the world less fortunate than we suffer not from a lack of democracy or principles (indeed most of them have a surfeit of one or the other) but from a lack of politics.

These are the kinds of problems that teacher-librarians face today.

1. Librarians are hired without teacher training.

2. Library clerks are taking over in libraries while teacher-librarians are being assigned classroom teaching and supervision duties. (In one district the last teacher-librarian was just phased out in favor of library clerks.)

3. "Standards" are not being recognized by administration.

4. Declining enrollment is resulting in teacher-librarians being moved back into the classroom.

5. Teachers are not in support of librarians' positions and have differing perceptions of the role of the teacher-librarian.

6. There is a lack of school board policies on libraries creating large variation in standards from district to district.

7. Teacher-librarians are being used to give preparation time to teachers. This is causing problems, tensions and a split in the ranks.

8. Teacher-librarians have varying attitudes toward their own role.

9. There is a general lack of space in school libraries due to increasing collections and additions of modern machines and equipment.

10. Teachers with no library qualifications are running school libraries.

The significant conclusion to be drawn of course is that most of these items concern not libraries per se but librarians. It may well be that the library has become part of the school but the librarian hasn't.

A 1980 school district questionnaire asked teachers to put top priority on items for the district's annual budget. A total of seven put "more time for librarians in small schools." I found out later that there were seven librarians in small schools. Seventy-three wanted reduced class sizes and that sort of thing. But quite a number of priorities listed things other than personal involvement. Only eight wanted average English classes of 25 though there were more than eight English teachers sampled. A number put answers concerning aides and support staff. The number advocating increased administrative support time was zero. The importance of this is to illustrate what I consider to be the very important differences in perception of need between teacher-librarians and other teachers. All is not well and perhaps politics and power can help.

Power is defined as "any person, body or thing having authority or influence." Note particularly the "or influence." In the political market place influence is often as important as authority. People do have power when they can make decisions that affect the lives of others. Who has power? Obviously those in authoritative positions. Not so obvious, but very important, are those who have power because people think they have it. What one might call the "illusion of power." Hobbes, the political theorist, said "power is the reputation of power." Secretary-treasurers of school districts operated by virtue of the illusion of power (and perhaps many still do). A school trustee once said to me, "But our secretary-treasurer wouldn't let us do that." A perfect illustration of real authority deferring to illusory authority.

A third type of person who has power is difficult to describe. They are the people—fairly rare—who have a capacity to make people believe in them. They are granted power by others. It is part charisma, part pecking order, part strength of purpose and clarity of goals. Their power is neither authoritative nor illusory. Some teacher-librarians do have it—they are in no danger of being replaced.

The last group has power because of their perceived importance in the scheme of things. They tend not to exercise power but influence it by their very existence and are a real constraint on other people's power. For example: If, as a newly appointed superintendent, I announced that I was about to declare redundant all Grade One teachers I would be taken away and become an object of interest to psychiatrists. But if I announced that the school system could not afford the luxury of qualified teacher-librarians, the news would in most districts I suspect be greeted with a great deal of disinterest and, what is worse, some librarians would not express any outrage.

There are constraints on power. We can skim over the more obvious traditional constraints—the law, the customs and mores of particular communities, financial constraints. Most important are the people constraints—again, the obvious one of people in authority, whether real or illusory, constraining the power of other people in authority and the one of people perceived by others as being important (Grade One teachers). The one I wish to stress is the constraint on power that is almost total when certain interests or groups get aroused. It is one thing to have disgruntled individuals or small groups, it is quite another to face the outrage of the profession or the public. That at times is the most potent political constraint on power.

Let me take you through the school system indicating who has power and what constraints there are on power. Most of it is obvious, but most people in the library business rarely if ever consider their work in a "political" context.

A mistake is commonly made of describing power solely in hierarchical terms—minister; boards; principals; teachers; kids—with everyone above telling everyone below what they are supposed to be doing. There's too much of this going on now which is one of the reasons teachers are under strain; there's too much clash between the expectations of society and directions from the top. But despite that it is better to describe the situation in Aristotelian terms than in purely hierarchical ones as shown in figure 1.

In this analysis of the school system and power, librarians are not included. Apart from a few rare people (because of personal dynamism) teacher-librarians have no power either through authority or by illusion (this is the unkindest cut of all). You are not viewed as important in the scheme of things, you are not a constraint on anyone else's power.

It is a sad commentary on our system of education. In my view the system does not appear to need teacher-librarians. It barely (and count this as a smashing victory) needs the libraries that you work in. The nostalgic reactionaries who have been occupying the most powerful positions in education, with their misplaced enthusiasm for compulsory courses and standardized tests, their tolerance for learning that becomes a mindless, regurgitating recital of inconsequentials, don't need libraries to make their system work and they need librarians even less. The system is closed and controlled. Libraries, the great record of people's triumphs and follies, open the mind. The system sorts and trains; libraries educate.

Lest I get too involved in taking pot shots at ministries of education, you can influence power. The suggestions fall into two categories: competence, and political action.

The library is not a subject but a service and most services are taken for granted until they are needed. The message is clear and simple. You must be needed more, and to do that you have to stress those aspects of your competence that involve your colleagues in the school and at the same time challenge the system of education which does not place a premium on discovery and inquiry and thus does not find much need for your services.

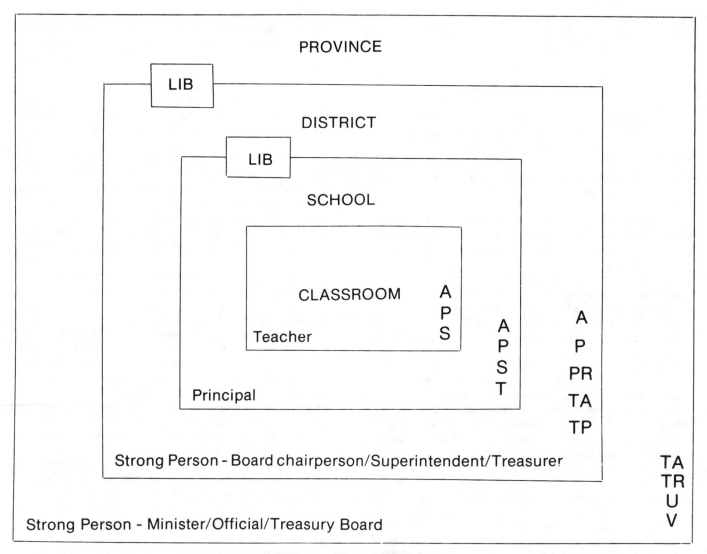

CONSTRAINTS ON POWER

A- AUTHORITIES
P- PARENTS
PR- PRESSURE GROUPS
S- STUDENTS
T- TEACHERS

TA- TEACHERS' ASSOCIATIONS
TP- TAX PAYERS
U- UNIVERSITIES
V- VOTERS

Fig. 1.

The emphasis in your work must be in areas of joint action, of teamwork, of direct involvement with the trials and tribulations of teachers. If you do that, you will be necessary and you will become a factor in the power business. If you don't, then I suspect we will see more of you replaced with a combination of machines and aides.

You also need to do a much better job of selling yourself and your wares. But again let that selling be done on the basis of the needs of kids and teachers. You should not sit and wait

for others to demand your services. The expectation of teachers is that at least 95 percent of what they do is ordained. You must get in there and challenge the system. You must be a teaching partner, not a sleeping partner!

Competence is the same as breathing, eating, sleeping, drinking. Without them I am nothing, but they are means to an end, not an end in itself. Competence as a librarian is only useful when it has influence on the mainstream of school life, which is what goes on between teacher and learner. You now need to develop a strong team approach with other teachers. Similarly, do not neglect parents. For educational and political reasons, encourage a great deal of contact particularly with parents of preschool children. Get them into your libraries.

If you have ever railed against the ignorance and parsimony of elected officials or their chief bureaucrats — and I don't know anybody in the library business who hasn't — you are wasting your breath and your energy. As a librarian in the system you have no power and about the same amount of influence. As an individual it is easy to concede defeat to "city hall" and become cynical about the political process. But you belong to groups that do matter; you're a taxpayer, maybe a parent, certainly you belong to a professional organization.

Well-organized groups can and do play a significant part in school board and municipal elections. You can do the same. Most local elections are patronized by a small percentage of the voters. The group that is best organized will win the day. Here is a recipe for political action:

1. Identify candidates with sensible ideas. Persuade them to run. Strong people, not Caspar Milquetoasts.

2. Pose the issues to all candidates to clear muddy waters.

3. Identify who is in the field. There are the nostalgic reactionaries with their chamber of commerce or "Happy Days" mentality. Their belief is that somewhere back in the 1950s the world was beautiful. They have this cockeyed folk memory that there was a time when all typists spelled perfectly, all shop attendants calculated correctly and all university students wrote impeccable essays, and if we just returned to the kind of school system we had in those days the world would come to its senses. Don't underestimate them, they have a powerful, appealing message that combines back to the basics with fiscal responsibility (and in some provinces 70 percent of taxpayers are nonparents).

   Romantic humanists. Probably most of you would fit into this category. Politically not terribly well-organized. Pedigree by Dewey out of Rousseau. Not hard-nosed enough when in power.

   Militant crusaders. (I sometimes call them Bloody Barbarians — when I'm feeling charitable.) Dangerous lot when they get into the field. God and quadratic equations. Everything else is a frill. Death on librarians. Cause teachers' federations to lower the drawbridge and gallop out to do battle. Normally the federations don't want to interfere in that political process but somebody has to defend the holy grail.

   The great stunned. The average citizens who have expectations (God bless them) that the system will produce out of their kids literate citizens with better jobs than they have. The other three groups try to get their votes.

4. Identify supporters. Now, when you have identified who is in the field, and I hope you can find a new type, a hard-nosed humanist, and your questions have identified the true colours of each candidate, you then have to identify your supporters, get the information to them, run a telephone campaign to "get out the vote" with the last call on polling day. Do not openly support any candidate. (You might be surprised at how effective it can be.)

Some co-operation between public and school librarians could be fruitful in the political arena. Think of all those lists of potential supporters each has access to.

Some of the same criteria apply with local teachers' associations. Unless there is a burning provincial or local issue, getting a quorum to meetings is always a problem. Finding people who will hold office is another one. Well-organized local librarians could get significant disproportionate representation at representative assemblies, annual general meetings and in local association offices, if they worked at it. Those positions can influence policy and thus influence the power brokers. The political system is alive and well — use it, don't complain about it.

At the provincial level the same tactics can be used in elections. You question the candidates on the issues that are important to you. They are aware that you are going to feed their responses into your network. You activate the network. Experts tell us that if you get to one person you have got to nine people because of family, kinship, recreational networks, and so on. A constituency with a thousand teachers or library supporters or whatever can be potentially influenced by your actions. Most elections are won or lost by a few thousand votes. The politicians know that. So should you. That's influence and an entirely legitimate enterprise. The business community, unions, the fish and game league, the gun lobby, you name it, all regard it as a necessary pursuit. They are in the marketplace with their needs and wants which they will achieve only in proportion to the degree of influence they can wield. Do you think that your cause is less worthy than any of those groups? Don't expect the political system to reward you without effort. Get out there and shake it up a bit.

There are forces in society that affect children and schools because they are germane to the topic of power and teacher-librarians. We are sometimes not fully aware of the momentous nature of the technological and scientific revolution we are undergoing. It has caused and is causing profound and significant changes in the social and economic pillars on which the school rests. Schools designed for one kind of industrial society have to cope with the human products of a different kind of society. So far the old industrial school has managed (with the assistance of those nostalgic reactionaries) to accommodate those forces at the cost of a great deal of stress for teachers because whatever the system demands makes no less real the pressures from the society in which the school is located.

The first pillar on which the school rests is employment. The old school was a screening device that sorted people out into the world of work and higher education. Dramatic shifts in the nature of employment from manual and semi-skilled to technical and service-oriented jobs have created the situation in which the papers are full of ads for jobs while the unemployment rate is at its highest level ever. More profoundly still, it has more than doubled the retention rate in schools. That simple statistic is in effect a revolutionary statistic. Between 1961 and 1971 the retention rate from Grades 2 to 12 in Canadian schools went from 36 percent to 71 percent. It is now about 80 percent. No other factor accounts for all the contradictory claims and counter-claims about educational performance and standards. The industrial school was designed to weed out, not to accommodate.

The second pillar is communications. Schools were savagely print-oriented and still are. The printing press made modern nationalism possible. What are the effects of instant communication, new forms of literacy, visual/computer literacy? The effects on language and the effects on attitudes in the social sciences will be most profound. The premises are there. So far we have resisted the challenge by crying about standards and English exams at the university level.

The third pillar is that the old school was based on a nuclear family home situation. The economic and sexual emancipation of women stemming from "the pill" is rapidly changing the family base for many children. The school is not immune and cannot remain aloof from these different circumstances.

Fourth, there has been a shift in values from consensus to pluralism. Perhaps this is a consequence of all the other changes. The old school rested on a stable value system. The new school has to try to satisfy all kinds of strongly held values and whatever the school does you can rest assured that it will be wrong for a vocal minority. In some school districts half of the children come from homes where English is the second language if it is spoken at all. Some schools have as many as eighteen languages heard on the playground at recess. If we are to preserve this marvellous mosaic we won't help that cause much with tests that measure the difference between 14.77 and 14.87 on a standardized English exam.

There are two major implications that I see for educators in all these changes. School programs must be designed to allow students to master the technology that is capable of dominating our lives, and they must reflect the aesthetic and human side of mankind or the technology with its powerful capacity for alienation will dominate us. Microcomputers are about to become as commonplace in schools as chalkboards. A little chip can contain the Encyclopedia Britannica. If I were running a school system these days I would bribe, coerce, kidnap teacher-librarians to force them to take computer courses. I never underestimate the ability of the school to absorb any revolutionary tool and put it in its place but I would be very wary of something that could take my library and encapsule it in something the size of the thumbnail and then instantly retrieve any part of it, given the right instructions. You have an opportunity to get in on the ground floor of what I believe must finally and drastically change the teaching/learning business. Seize that opportunity or you will live to regret it.

Second, the other side of the technological coin is its ability to alienate while performing useful services. Our schools must stress, much more than they do now, those things of the mind and spirit that are creative, that have the potential to provide some balance.

Teacher-librarians working with teachers can have a unique influence on students and on education. Years ago I used to stump about the country preaching that the library should take over the school. If anything, I hold to that belief more firmly than I did then. The stressing of specialized teaching competence will make your work necessary to others and political strategies and seizing control of the technological tools that will soon dominate our classrooms, will get you into the stream of power. With this, nothing is more important than the task to speak loudly and boldly for children. The libraries in which you work contain the cultural history of mankind. Who else has a better case for being involved in the educational process? What you treasure and what you do should so affect the lives of teachers and students that, in Carlyle's elegant phrase, you "help students become all that they are capable of becoming."

Too Many Chickens ... Too Few Hogs

Lorne MacRae

Recently, at a meeting of school librarians, great venting of spleen occurred when the participants vociferously shared the concern that adult education students using the schools at night were a disruptive element to the day program. Night school teachers used equipment cavalierly and frequently wanted to borrow support materials from the school library. Rather than explore possibilities for making a frustrating experience a positive one in which school librarians would shine as the purveyors of library glitter to an already beleaguered potential group of users, the school librarians wanted to explore ways of saying "No" to the media-hungry night school teachers. Reflecting upon this gives rise to the thought that Pogo was right—"we have found the enemy and he is us"—and that the crisis in Canadian school librarianship is the average Canadian school librarian.

The fact remains, in spite of booming circulation figures, that Canadian school librarianship is in a general state of decline frequently in spite of ourselves and frequently because of ourselves! It isn't the direct fault of the hassled school librarians with the night school problem that they are unable to address the problem effectively. But they must share much of the indirect blame. Surely, by extending school library services to school populations not normally served, it would be possible to create another climate of acceptability for school library programs in general. It is in the collective understanding of what a school library program is that much of the problem exists. A school library program is a vision, an extension—it is the integration of media with curriculum and the sophisticated mental processes required to synthesize knowledge and produce an articulate outpouring of opinion and belief that encapsulates the essence of a school library program. Recent issues of the *Mocassin Telegraph* point out the diminishing numbers of school librarians in Canada. Recent issues of the *Wilson Library Bulletin* indicate that the same is true in the United States. Such decline is indeed a by-product of our inability to address the bureaucracies with which we find ourselves embroiled. We are unable to lobby effectively in either of the main institutions that should provide us with support.

Given the historical development of school libraries in Canada the past 20 years have been the blossoming years. When school libraries started the school librarian ordered, catalogued, inventoried, produced statistics, and so forth. This perception of service is the perception of most senior administrators who were either young teachers or old students during the developmental years. To convince these administrators of the need for full-time school librarians, adequate support staff, and appropriate budget is a monumental task. But it requires positive vision and not negative protectionism. Compounding the problem is the fact that school librarians, because they are certificated teachers, also exist under the umbrella of a teacher association. Unfortunately, the same perceptions of school library service are shared by many of the administrators that guide the helm of these ships. One such

teacher association has for many years given lip service to the concept of school library service and the requirements to provide such service. It is interesting to note that this same association maintains a professional library staffed by a library technician. If a library technician can serve the needs of the association's central staff, and fill phone and mail requests to outlying jurisdictions, then it is not difficult to presume that this association could also by default permit the role of the school librarian to become that of a library technician. A realigning of research skills into the Social Studies program or Language Arts program makes it plausible and possible.

School librarians need to form vocal groups that do not require the established bureaucratic process in order to speak. Too often school librarians, having noted a concern, must wait for a year (or longer) while their association bureaucracy possibly salutes their concern and then enacts impotent action to right the wrong. School librarians must align themselves with organizations that can speak directly to the educational power-brokers. It is vitally important for school librarians to join the Chamber of Commerce, the Junior League, the Lions, Kiwanis, and so forth. School librarians should get elected to the boards of the societies that control the opera, theatre, ballet, athletic associations, as examples. Frequently the people on the boards come into direct contact with the political educational decision makers. If school librarians are unable to attack the problems frontally, then it is best to do so by indirect association.

However, the key to the problem is whether or not school librarians en masse, or even in a largish number, really do have a fighting conviction that school libraries are an important educational dimension in the school, and that the demise of the school library would be a mortal wound from which the educational patient might not survive. Unless this conviction is shared, then those who do lobby are battling not only the unknowing but also their own complacent colleagues. The spin-off effect devastates the eager. There is no room for complacency in the field of school librarianship in Canada today. More school librarians are being asked to teach classes in subject areas, supervise classes, work with reduced support staff, provide the same up-to-date information after budget cuts, and still provide the same level of service. Some will persevere and work longer hours. They will lobby and fight. They will cajole and convince. But it is difficult to convince a system, a district or a province when some school libraries close 10 minutes after the school bell rings, when an extended lunch hour for the school librarian excludes service to students bussed to the school, or when an overdue list is more important than a session of unit planning. For every school librarian that fights the philosophic battle, based on an active program of service, there are others who pray that further intrusions into the school library concept will not force them back into the classroom from which they originally sought refuge. It is for the fighters to continue the fight—they must not permit themselves the luxury of weariness. They must, however, permit themselves the luxury of relationships with like-fellows, and develop intellectual horizons that refresh; read, attend theatre productions, visit art galleries, climb mountains, and sail windy lakes ... and when refreshed, continue what seems to be a solitary fight and a lonely battle. But others are looking toward the same goal. There is solace in that!

The CSLA will hopefully become a viable political force in spite of the difficult provincial educational scene in Canada. However, counterproductive relationships must be removed or altered. Where is the CSLA implementation kit designed to promote *Resource Services for Canadian Schools?* A creative venture has been stymied by a counterproductive relationship that has prevented "Irons from striking while hot!" Politically active school librarians have traditionally been able to work quickly, when permitted to solve problems. This must not be denigrated by those who would linger over apostrophes. The CSLA must re-address the ways in which it wants to deliver its message to its perceived clientele and deliver to that clientele the means for them to lobby their clientele. Not only must we

save our seals, and whales, and Siberian tigers, and silver darters, we must also save our school librarians ... not for ourselves but for the real educational program that can occur when the dedicated, committed school librarian is able to perform without constantly looking back to see if some budgetary or philosophic axe is about to fall.

The key to the whole crisis in Canadian school librarianship is with the commitment of school librarians themselves. They must not say as did Chief Joseph of the Nez Percé Indian, "I will fight no more forever," but rather like Churchill maintain that the fight has just begun and strike an attitude of—"of course we'll win." Frederick Wagman, former librarian at the University of Michigan, said to the 1967 School of Librarianship graduating class that librarians have to make a decision about their commitment to the profession. They must decide whether that commitment is total or partial. He likened this commitment to the relationship the hog and the chicken have to the bacon and eggs breakfast. The commitment of the chicken is partial and that of the hog, total! The crisis in Canadian school librarianship is that there are too many chickens and too few hogs.

Hard Times ... Hard Choices

Ken Haycock

In times of declining financial support for public institutions and services of all kinds it is perhaps useful to remind ourselves of the basic principles on which school library services thrive and prosper and the major issues confronting the profession. Too often we deal well with the symptoms but ignore the causes, resulting in an inevitable rematch, as symptoms, like weeds, keep coming up.

The research and the experience of those developing support for teacher-librarians and school resource centres, is quite clear. The single most important role of the teacher-librarian is cooperative program planning and teaching with classroom teachers. This major shift for the teacher-librarian from determining what the student is to do, to cooperatively determining what the student is to learn, has resulted in the teacher becoming the primary focus. Cooperative planning and team teaching not only provide better opportunities for purposeful use of library resources and the integration of media, research and study skills with classroom instruction but also provide better opportunities for classroom teachers and administrators to learn first hand the role of the teacher-librarian as a teaching partner, something quite different from a teaching adjunct. The need for *flexible scheduling* of facilities and services is obvious if integration is to take place. Furthermore, it is downright foolish for the school's librarian to provide planning/preparation time for teachers if the first priority of the teacher-librarian is to be available to plan with

that teacher. Some school districts have policies defining clearly the role of the teacher-librarian and mandating flexible scheduling of resource centres. (There *are* cheaper ways to provide spare periods for teachers!) Teacher-librarians need a defined role, the integrity and confidence to stand by it and a willingness to take risks in initiating planning with colleagues.

Needless to say, teacher-librarians need the skills of *program advocacy*. It is essential that both school and district personnel and decision-makers understand the "newer" role of the teacher-librarian and its importance for teaching and learning. Every teacher-librarian should be able to articulate the aim of the program (see *Emergency Librarian*, 8:5), the best means of achieving that aim, the role of principals and teachers in a *cooperative* venture, and the confidence to talk to parent and community groups, professional groups and individuals about these. Put simply, if the teacher-librarian doesn't sell the program, nobody will and it *is* a given that teachers have no idea of the role of the teacher-librarian at the beginning of their careers.

And how well prepared is the teacher-librarian for these roles? *Education for school librarianship* holds the key to both success and survival in school librarianship but where are the courses (not a single class) in cooperative planning? It isn't good enough any more to direct prospective teacher-librarians to work with teachers—how do you do it? What are the curricular entry points? the strategies for involvement? the skills to work with professionals you dislike? the scope and sequence of research and study skills K-12? the process for developing school-based policies? Where are the courses in cooperative teaching in elementary and secondary schools? When are the professional skills of in-service education for teachers taught and applied? Where are the strategies for implementing innovation dealt with? Since new courses are unlikely to be added, teacher-librarians will have to continue to argue for a restructuring of existing programs to better meet needs identified by both the profession and research.

It's time to stand up and be counted as a professional with integrity, confidence and skill. The management of newer materials and technology, while important, will not save or even necessarily enhance the status of the teacher-librarian if undertaken outside this framework. The future lies in working closely with teachers within the context of a clearly defined role, understood and advocated by teacher-librarians and thus by administrators, teachers and the community.

Part 3
THE STRATEGIES

A few definitions may be in order by way of introduction:

advocacy—the action of arguing or pleading for a cause

change—to pass from one phase to another and make different in some particular way

collegiality—the relationship and shared responsibility of associates

consensus—general agreement representing the collective opinion arrived at by those concerned

influence—the power exerted over others through position, intellect, force of character or degree of accomplishment, thus producing an effect in indirect ways, without apparent exertion of tangible force

jargon—special vocabulary used by a particular group, often pretentious and unnecessarily obscure

lobbying—making personal contact and/or disseminating information to influence decision-makers

marketing—moving ideas and services from the producer to the consumer

power—capable of producing an effect

public relations—the promotion of reciprocal understandings and goodwill between an individual or institution and other persons, special publics or the community at large, including the distribution of interpretive material

publicity—any effort to attract public attention and interest whether through the dissemination of information and promotional material or paid advertising

**The product is eminently worthwhile and, buttressed by a
solid commitment, the strategies become much more feasible
taken one step at a time.**

If You Don't Know What's Important
Then Everything Is Important

If Everything Is Important
Then You Try To Do Everything

If You Are Attempting To Do Everything
Then People Will Expect
You To Do Everything

And In Trying To Please Everyone
You Don't Have Enough Time
To Find Out What's Important

The Teacher-Librarian and Planned Change

Linda Rehlinger

INTRODUCTION

All programs and positions in the public school system come under close scrutiny, but this is especially true for those teachers whose responsibilities lie outside the "bare essential," the self-contained classroom. In times of restraint in particular, teacher-librarians may be faced with changes in assignments which are unplanned and unwelcome. These changes can vary from the reduction of assigned teacher-librarian time, to reassignment to another position, to termination of the teacher-librarian position altogether. As a group, teacher-librarians have not been effective advocates of their role in the education of students. "It may well be that the library has become part of the school but the librarian hasn't."[1:6] As a group, teacher-librarians are now discovering the absolute necessity of becoming not only skilled advocates of their unique contribution within the system, but also of becoming effective change agents within the school organization.

The purpose here is to identify a model of planned organizational change that could be applied in school situations, to illustrate the "fit" between the model and the situation of the individual teacher-librarian, and to describe a modified action plan that could be used by teacher-librarians in order to promote planned change.

THE ACTION RESEARCH MODEL OF PLANNED ORGANIZATIONAL CHANGE

Action research considers planned change as a cyclical rather than a linear process. It is characterized by a heavy emphasis on data gathering and diagnosis before the planning and implementation of any actions. It typically consists of seven main steps that are carried out in a continuous cycle:[8]

- problem identification by a key individual

- consultation with a behavioral science expert

- data gathering and preliminary diagnosis

- feedback to the key client or group

- joint diagnosis of the problem

- action

- data gathering after the action

Organizations that are experiencing problems can usually be classed as either "overorganized" or "underorganized." Overorganized situations are characterized by policies, procedures, leadership, organizational structure, and job descriptions that are too rigid and overly defined for effective task performance; in underorganized situations the opposite is true. In the latter, leadership, structure, job design and policy are ill-defined and fail to control task behaviors effectively. As a result, communication flows are fragmented, job responsibilities are ambiguous, and energies are dissipated because of lack of direction.

The seven steps are appropriate for effecting change in an overorganized situation where the degree of organization needs to be loosened; the underorganized situation, which needs the degree of organization to be tightened, requires a different scenario. The desired result in this case would include increasing the amount of organization by clarifying roles, structuring communication lines between parties, and specifying job responsibilities. The stages of this plan are:[8]

- identification of the parties concerned

- the "convention": getting everyone together

- creation of organizing mechanisms — new procedures and policies

- evaluation

ACTION RESEARCH AND THE TEACHER-LIBRARIAN

The current status of teacher-librarians in the educational system is analogous, on an individual level, to that of the "underorganized" system of the action research model: job responsibilities that are ambiguous; communication flows that are fragmented; energies that are dissipated.

Ambiguous Job Responsibilities

There appears to be a lack of agreement as to just what constitutes the teacher-librarian's job. Many reports[2,6,7] indicate that principals and teachers both have fairly clear, though conflicting, ideas on the role of the teacher-librarian. Principals see teacher-librarians as having a strong professional role in curriculum affairs, while teachers see them as experts at clerical and technical tasks. There is no such widespread agreement, however, among teacher-librarians; confusion is rampant about the relative importance and melding of the two aspects of the role, that of the materials organizer and the teacher of research and information skills. This is further complicated by the fact that while the organizational and managerial tasks must be done in order for the collection to be accessible, levels of clerical help have been drastically cut during restraint; teacher-librarians are now often doing clerical tasks rather than supervising them.

A clear understanding of role definitions is critical in order for social institutions like schools to operate successfully.[4] Role expectations consistent with these definitions can then follow. It would seem, therefore, that a clear and acceptable role definition for the teacher-librarian in each school is needed. Until this occurs, it is unlikely that the teacher-librarian can become a truly successful advocate for school resource centers and have any influence on program and staffing decisions.

Fragmented Communication

One of the obvious ramifications of ambiguous job responsibilities is fragmented and ineffective communication. If you don't know what you're supposed to be doing, how can you promote those policies and services? If teacher-librarians demonstrate this characteristic of an underorganized system, one would expect to find that the inability to articulate philosophy and services would be evident. Indeed, the literature does indicate that teacher-librarians do not, as a group, communicate effectively to either principals or teachers.[6] Considering the volume of published material on interpersonal communication techniques, and the apparent need for these skills by teacher-librarians, there seems to be a decided scarcity in the literature of school librarianship of practical applications of these techniques for the teacher-librarian.

Even with individuals who are skilled in communication techniques, there are blocks that crop up in the system. One of these is a reduction of the time available for planning and information sessions with individual teachers; this is often caused not only by a decrease in the amount of preparation time for teachers (coupled with an increased teaching load), but also by a reduction in the teacher-librarian's time. The teacher-librarian's supervision duties in the resource center (often before school, at noon, and after school) may seriously limit the times available to be with colleagues socially while gently "spreading the word." Reductions in inservice opportunities, a fact of life in many districts due to budget cuts, can further hamper communication. Finally, communication can be fragmented if conflicting messages come from the teacher-librarian and the school administrator. In a case like this, the teacher-librarian almost always loses, as the research shows that the "principal is the single most important factor in the development of a strong library program."[7]

Energy Dissipation

The final characteristic of the underorganized situation is that the energy of employees is dissipated due to a lack of direction. This "directionlessness" conjures up images of the individual bouncing from one unpriorized activity to the next—the scenario of teacher-librarian as the ball in the pinball machine. There is a further implication that energies are not only expended in many directions, but they are also expended fruitlessly. This is the kind of environment in which "burn-out" flourishes. Is the energy of the teacher-librarian dissipated? Is burn-out a concern in the community of teacher-librarians?

Lyn Street[9] delightfully summarizes the dissipation of teacher-librarian energy through thirty-five roles (apart from "teacher" and "librarian") that the teacher-librarian is called upon to fill, from equipment coordinator to professional reader to publicist to clairvoyant. While amusing and light in tone, Street's writing underscores the dangers of energy dissipation which are, indeed, there. Without a clear sense of role, these demands cannot be evaluated and ranked as to their importance to the overall program.

One would expect that if energy dissipation were a problem, then burn-out among teacher-librarians would be a concern. A search of the literature indicates that burn-out is a problem, and it is of recent origin. Prior to 1981, only one original article existed in the literature; since then, eleven articles about teacher-librarians and burn-out have been written.[5] It is not surprising that teacher-librarians should be at risk along with the other helping professions, as they encounter the four organizational stressors that lead to burn-out—role ambiguity, role overload (too much work), role insufficiency (not enough time or materials), and responsibility for others.[3]

A MODIFIED ACTION RESEARCH PLAN FOR TEACHER-LIBRARIANS

If the situation of teacher-librarians is analogous to the underorganized system of the action research model, then the action research plan for those systems (identification of the affected parties; convening of the individuals; the creation of new organizing mechanisms; evaluation) would be an appropriate plan. However, there is a factor in the organization of a school system that is not taken into account by the underorganized model. This is the power and authority of the principal of the school. The principal has a real and legitimate authority concerning the operation of the school, and cannot be bypassed by any change model that hopes to be successful. Therefore, step one from the "overorganized" action plan (problem identification by a key individual) might become step one of the modified action research plan. In fact, the key individual to identify a problem concerning the resource center may be the teacher-librarian but regardless of where the idea arose, the principal will have to be convinced that there is a problem before any action plan can be put into effect. It is best if the principal gives wholehearted support to necessary change or, at the very least, sanctions the procedure.

EXAMPLE

The Setting:

Washington Elementary School enrolls 400 students K-7. It has 19 staff members and 14 classes; there is a full-time principal, learning assistance teacher, and teacher-librarian. The average age of the staff is 45, and none has less than 10 years teaching experience. The former teacher-librarian moved after spending 20 years in the school. She prided herself on keeping the resource center neat and inviting, and enjoyed her scheduled library times with each class. She had heard of the concept of cooperative program planning and teaching, but considered it an innovation that would go the way of the open area school. The principal had also heard rumblings of "new ideas in using libraries," but did not consider it important enough to buck the opposition of the teacher-librarian and the lack of knowledge of the staff. Only five staff members had ever worked closely with a teacher-librarian. Joan Masters, the new teacher-librarian, is eager to have a flexibly scheduled resource center and to begin planning and teaching with the staff.

Step #1:
Problem Identification by a Key Individual

Joan Masters must first convince the principal that the changes she wants to instigate are worthwhile. She might encourage communication with her previous principal or with others from her former staff, or from other schools, those whose opinions would be highly regarded.

She should ask for an appointment so that she can communicate to the principal her conception of the role of the teacher-librarian, and outline the kinds of things that she has done in the past that she thinks are valuable for staff and students.

She could outline the kinds of changes that she would like to see and ask if the principal could lend his support to the concept of service that she would like to provide.

Only when she has this concept support from the principal can she ask to lead a staff workshop to clarify role expectations.

Step #2:
Identification of the Parties Concerned

The classroom teachers are obvious choices, but the learning assistance teacher should also be included, as well as any teacher aides who work with students. In addition, any itinerant teachers who might possibly be involved in classroom activities should be invited. It is critical that the principal be present during the workshop session as this presence indicates approval of a willingness for change.

Groundwork should be laid with the staff.

Step #3:
The Convention (Workshop/Discussion/Idea Session)

This will be an introduction to the topic of how the resource center and teacher-librarian might be used in the school. It should be presented as a non-threatening, information-gathering session that will focus on the ways that this staff would like to use the particular skills of the new teacher-librarian.

Given the background, it would probably be wise to start with an individual activity where people list all the jobs that they think a teacher-librarian can and should do. (Or, they can be provided with ideas, plus space for additions, if their level of awareness seems particularly low.) They then could divide into small groups (three or so), and amalgamate and rank their lists. Two groups then join and go through the procedure again. The groups then chart and display their ideas. A discussion should then ensue about the order of the ideas; the teacher-librarian should try to focus attention on ranking first the things that would be of most benefit to them in their teaching programs (especially with regard to teaching research and information skills).

A general summation should now be made by the teacher-librarian outlining the consensus of the group about the type of resource center services that they perceive that they want. (This can be the start of a policy statement.)

At this time, the teacher-librarian should explain her perceptions of the role of the teacher-librarian, stressing any points of convergence with the staff's views. Ideas about new procedures and techniques should be introduced at this point, always stressing the benefits to the individual teacher's program and students. It may be helpful at this time, depending on the staff, to have a person from the previous school describe how they worked cooperatively with the teacher-librarian, and why they liked it.

The teacher-librarian might then ask for volunteers to work on a committee with her. The purpose of this committee would be to get on paper a draft set of procedures that would be presented to the staff for acceptance on a trial basis. For the greatest chance of successful change, try to get the principal and a true cross-section of teacher-opinion on the committee.

Step #4:
The Creation of the Organizing Mechanisms

Meet with the committee to draft the new procedures and proposed policies for presentation to the staff for adoption.

Present the procedures to the staff. Discussion will follow, and possibly adoption on a trial basis. If agreement cannot be reached, it must go back to the committee stage, with the inclusion of the person with the most qualms on the committee. It is important that staff have "ownership" of the planned changes.

Re-submission to the staff. Acceptance. Implementation begins.

Step #5:
Evaluation

This must be a continuous monitoring of how things are going, with meetings with sub-groups or the whole group as needed to iron out any problems. At any time, any staff member could initiate step #1: again by identifying a problem.

CONCLUSION

A modified action research plan fits the reality of the school organization in which teacher-librarians work. If used, it offers an opportunity for planned, constructive, and lasting change concerning the use of school resource centers and the services of teacher-librarians. However, this plan, or any other, will only work for teacher-librarians if each one takes personal responsibility for completing professional specialist training and developing both a well-considered personal philosophy on cooperative program planning and teaching and a sure sense of the role of the teacher-librarian in the education system.

BIBLIOGRAPHY

1. Bowman, Jim. "Power and the School Librarian—Starting Here, Starting Now." *Emergency Librarian*, Volume 9, Number 1 (September-October, 1981), pages 6-11.

2. Burdenuk, Gene. "Who Speaks for Us? Power, Advocacy and the Teacher-Librarian." *Emergency Librarian*, Volume 11, Number 3 (January-February, 1984), pages 18-22.

3. Eskridge, Denise. "Teacher Stress: Symptoms, Causes and Management Techniques." *The Clearing House*, Volume 58, Number 9 (May, 1985) pages 387-90.

4. Gue, Leslie R. *An Introduction to Educational Administration in Canada*. Second edition. McGraw, 1985.

5. Haack, Mary. "Occupational Burnout among Librarians." *Drexel Library Quarterly*, Volume 20, Number 2 (Spring, 1984), pages 46-72.

6. Hambleton, Alixe. "Static in the Educational Intercom—Conflict and the School Librarian." *Emergency Librarian*, Volume 9, Number 5 (May-June 1982), pages 18-20.

7. Haycock, Ken. "Strengthening the Foundations for Teacher-Librarianship." *School Library Media Quarterly*, Volume 13, Number 2 (Spring, 1985), pages 102-9.

8. Huse, Edgar and Thomas Cummings. *Organizational Development and Change*. West, 1985.

9. Street, Lyn. "The Teacher-Librarian as Polymath: Wonderwoman, Where Are You?" *The Bookmark*, Volume 22, Number 1 (September, 1980), pages 23-26.

Teacher-Librarian Collegiality: Strategies for Effective Influence

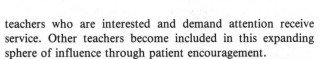

Ronald Jobe

Establishing relationships in today's world is increasingly challenging whether it is between two people or amongst staff members. A societal barrage of slogans such as, 'Don't get involved,' or 'Do your own thing' makes this even more difficult. People appear to be constantly too busy to set aside time for others. Relationships work only when people take the time to care about one another. It is as true for a teacher-librarian and staff, or a teacher and students.

It is important to be realistic in developing relations with a staff. Not every teacher will be enamored with the teacher-librarian. This fact should not cause undue distress because there can be many reasons for this apparent lack of enthusiasm: poor past experiences, pressures resulting from challenging class situations, or lack of awareness of the potential for school libraries. It should also be noted that service cannot possibly be given on an equal basis in a large school. Those teachers who are interested and demand attention receive service. Other teachers become included in this expanding sphere of influence through patient encouragement.

It is of the utmost importance for teacher-librarians to have established their personal resource centre philosophy, to be confident in themselves as people, to be self-reliant as teachers, and to be innovative, enthusiastic members of the staff. This is the first premise of successfully relating to colleagues. Be secure in yourself and be assertive about your professional privileges and responsibilities.

Collegiality involves being one of the teachers. It demands a sense of presence. The resource centre should be the focal point of activity for teacher-librarians. However, to increase their visibility and availability they should be using the entire school as a resource facility. This includes undertaking such activities as teaching in a classroom, having coffee in the staff room, visiting a teacher to see a new project, or talking to the children on the playground.

Acceptance of the teacher-librarian as a teacher is crucial to cooperative teaching. Muttered lamentations reflecting moans of rejection often do more harm than good. Such complaining does not usually achieve the desired results. However, honest reactions to events often bring staff understanding. Mutual exhaustion at the end of a hectic day, the need for coffee on certain mornings, and the innate pleasure of success will give credence to the evidence that teacher-librarians are colleagues too!

More things are achieved over a cup of coffee than are ever achieved at staff meetings! Insignificant as this statement may appear, it harbours a simple truth: teacher-librarians have to be where the action is. Inevitably the relief centre of the school is the staff room. A place for the whole staff to relax, blow off steam, express irritations, as well as to laugh at themselves. Physical presence makes one part of the mood of the moment and contributes to being looked upon by the staff as 'one of us.' What better place to become aware of what is really happening in the school than the staff room? An alert observer will make note of the expressed problems, frustrations, and desires of the staff for future action.

Whose resource centre is it? Each person in the school should feel free to state that this is 'our' resource centre. One small word can make an enormous difference in the teachers' perception of school resources. A sense of belonging develops when the teacher-librarian openly encourages the mutual selection and utilization of materials. This sense of unity evolves into a commitment to the success of the school resource program. However, the advancement of this program is determined by the positive image which the teacher-librarian projects. This image must reflect a focus of the teacher-librarian as an active participant in the educational program of the school.

What is your image? Only you can change it. What do the teachers on staff really see you doing? Do they actually see you or are you merely a part of the wall decor? Now is the time to consider some strategies which might elicit new spheres of influence for you.

STRATEGIES FOR EFFECTIVE INFLUENCE

Active Listener

You must *make time* for the important things! An observation of the time spent on your activities will be a fairly accurate indicator of your current priorities. Make time to listen. A sympathetic listener is needed in every school. Teachers as well as students have to have someone to talk with, to share their joys, frustrations, problems and defeats.

Complimentor

What every school needs too is a person who cares enough to offer genuine praise where it is deserved. People blossom with compliments. Tension is relieved and they think of themselves in more positive terms. Often teachers will continue to

pass such compliments on to their peers and to their students. Such action, although worthy in its own respect, also brings rewards because of the fact that you appear to be more open and approachable.

Written compliments are also most appreciated. When was the last time you wrote a colleague a thank you note for a favour done, or for sharing materials? Don't forget to write to a class of students, the principal, or a parent, too. The effect of such thoughtfulness can be quite overwhelming. Who should you write to today?

Environmental Designer

You can control the school's environment. Simply look around you—do you like to work in such an atmosphere? If not, change it! No you don't have to do all the work, merely provide the opportunity for others to help.

Three swift suggestions for immediate changes include the following:

A. Use colour boldly, plentifully, and freely. Students and teachers are very aware of colours and a duo-colour (red-yellow, blue-brown) is most tantalizing.

B. A little from many creates a lot! If each class contributes only two or three drawings or book characters, you'll have a multitude of sharings.

C. Plan ahead. Teachers like to have two to three weeks notice so that they can plan too! Surprises are just not appreciated.

Start with the resource centre and then gradually flow along the halls. Take over the bulletin boards immediately for visual vitality, then use display cabinets to share hobbies, collections, or travel souvenirs. Always include books and AV materials in these displays to stimulate resource centre use.

Curiosity Coordinator

What's this? Who's eye? Can you see it? How small is small? You are able to enrich the lives of the students who come to the resource centre by asking stimulating questions, creating high interest displays and evolving thought-provoking activities. If the children are from rather uncreative, non risk-oriented classrooms, stimulating curiosity about the exciting facts in books, making literature live, and sharing an enthusiasm for reading will all contribute to opening up new vistas. Success is achieving a glint in the eyes! Special attention should be given to making sessions both interesting and enjoyable for teachers, too! If the teacher wants to return the children will certainly be there as well.

Free Agent

Giving unrequested service proves to be a surprisingly effective means to arouse reluctant resource centre users. It proves that you are with it, know what's happening, and are concerned with each teacher individually. You must keep alert to current classroom projects, types of materials the teachers and students are borrowing, as well as current news events. In essence a major strategy to develop is that of being a professional eavesdropper! Overhearing comments made during informal conversations allows you to become aware of colleagues' needs without their realizing it. You then appear to be a mind reader!

Sustained "Ideator"

Teachers frequently need a shot in the arm. New ideas in small doses are always welcome. If you don't think up ideas readily, you might devise a collection of ideas which you keep for just this purpose. Quick one period art activities, language arts game ideas, crossword puzzles, mysterious science activities, or geography clues are most applicable. You must also maximize your use of periodicals. Quickly skim new issues for articles and ideas which might appeal to individual teachers. The time spent writing quick notes to colleagues will prove to be most beneficial, especially if you let two or more teachers know about the same article!

Library Promoter

Teachers are paid to read! You should take it as a challenge to motivate your colleagues to open a book! If they already read try to expand their reading tastes and interests. The only way to get staff members interested in books is to talk about them, preferably in a crowded staff room. Borrow books from colleagues and then quickly return them along with your comments. These informal book discussions often spur others to read too! Make books visible for the teachers by casually leaving them lying around on the staff room tables. Did you ever think to put some in the washrooms? Explosive results are assured—at least they'll be noticed!!

Avid Articulator

One of your most effective strategies is to be able to exhibit a high degree of oral competency within the staff. Always insist on a regular time during each staff meeting for a resource centre report. This must be an enthusiastic sharing of the program including new skill sessions to be offered, possible followup activities to storytelling, as well as recently arrived materials. Be sufficiently courageous to give book talks. Relate good books for children as well as those books in the collection which are of interest to adults.

Corner the consultants or visiting specialists in your school. These people are usually full of ideas and suggestions. Sharing this information with the staff sharpens your curricular awareness and gives you a point of departure for discussing school programs.

How are you at answering children's questions? We always need to improve this skill. Do you actually answer the question? Do you give sufficient specific information? Do you overtalk? Listen to yourself!

Colourful verbal barrages against much of the required 'donkey' work of a resource centre even serves to educate teachers into the 'secret' activities of teacher-librarians. Mutual respect evolves when teachers realize that you have a heavy work load too!

Skills Exemplar

Don't forget that your image must include an expertise in research skills. Show it! Take every opportunity to get involved with the teachers and students in their practical assignments.

Volunteer your services to teach a specific skill such as the use of the thesaurus or note taking from an encyclopedia. Remember that you are often instructing teachers, too!

Individual research projects with either eager or reluctant youngsters are a grand opportunity to exhibit what can really be achieved when individual needs are recognized. These youngsters, who have themselves experienced success, can consequently serve as tutors for their peers. You become a successful skills promoter only when you can show the purposeful integration of research skills into subject areas. Teachers must see the direct value of taking time to focus on skill ability, before they will integrate such practices into their teaching styles.

Theme Planner

That's a great idea!
  And you could also include...
  Did you think about...
  Why don't we try it?

You start simply with sincere interest and your eager enthusiasm continues to captivate your colleagues into becoming involved. It's crucial that you include yourself in the planning and participation of such themes.

The duration of thematic units can be one class period, one day, a week, or even a month. Success will often extend the time interval. Single focus sessions could highlight on the students' interests in crazy hats, underground war movements, great disasters, explosive moments in history, or indeed musicians alive today. Special days can be a "Salute to Edith Cavell, Helen Keller, or Florence Nightingale." 'I'm Blue!' might motivate a colour day with everybody wearing blue clothing and acting blue! A week of mystery, mice, or outer-space creatures can be followed by glimpses of aardvarks, King Tut, or magnetic attractiveness!

Each theme can include a selection of book talks, slides, pictures, poetry, excerpts from novels, related eyewitness accounts, art prints, music, realia, or sharings of personal experiences. The secret is for you to start out conservatively with small units and build on each successful happening. It won't be long before you are literally exploding with special events!

Curriculum Architect

The most complex, time consuming, intellectually demanding yet rewarding strategy that you can undertake is to design an aspect of curriculum. This is usually done with a team of teachers sufficiently in advance so as to allow time for establishing objectives, searching for resources, detailed planning, and integrating subject areas. A good starting point is to challenge your co-workers to try to make a routine topic more stimulating and enriching not only for the students but also for themselves. The Middle Ages, astronomy, urban redevelopment, pollution, sports psychology, nutrition, China, and survival of the oceans all offer imaginative possibilities for fresh approaches. This strategy is our ultimate goal, but it is only possible after you have successfully established a resource program and have achieved the confidence of your fellow teachers.

Collegiality? It's up to you! Only you can establish mutual bonds of respect, admiration, and influence between the teachers and yourself. No one can do it for you. Determine which strategies are successful for you now and try to adopt new ones. Frankly, you can't start any sooner in life than today!

On Jargon

Ken Haycock

As I sat and marvelled at the intricacies of the latest automated circulation system, I was struck by the comments of the librarians present. One was thrilled by the advent of "automated circ" while another asked about the handling of "pams." A more program-oriented participant queried the presenters on the effects on "BI." No one seemed the least bit concerned that the purpose of the presentation was to introduce new systems to members of the community who were also present. One brave soul finally asked what "circ" actually was (circulation) while others tackled the rest (pamphlets; bibliographic instruction!). I began to wonder again why librarians feel their star rising when they can obfuscate the obvious or shroud it in the mystery of jargon.

There are just so many ways by which we confuse or alienate our clients, whether teachers, students, or the general public. What on earth is a "pam" to the user? And then we tell them that they are stored in "vertical files," I suppose to distinguish them from horizontal files, whatever they are. Why do we insist on "periodicals" for what the rest of the world calls magazines? We can keep our distinctions between magazines and journals, and newsletters and serials, for ourselves, but why thrust this on the wary user?

In schools this becomes even more serious since the primary clients are our colleagues, with whom we share a common training and experience. Why then the references to "library skills?" As one teacher said, the only library skills he could think of were dusting and shelving—not terribly useful social skills! Library skills denote the basics of how to use a library, taught in the library, by the librarian. On the other hand, research and study skills, which are included in many curriculum guides as the responsibility of the classroom teacher, include the same things as we talk about, but in a manner which makes sense to other teachers and students. Most of the elements of so-called library skills are not specific to libraries at all, but simply components of information handling.

And what is the library program? If the role of the school librarian is based on partnerships, primarily through cooperative program planning and team teaching, how can there be a separate library program? Surely we are talking about resource-based learning, designed and implemented by teachers and librarians together.

This of course brings us to the library. Or the library media centre. Everyone knows about libraries—thus everyone knows about school libraries. But the services and traditions of public and academic libraries stress information access and delivery. School libraries, on the other hand, stress information processing and use. This difference in the basic tenet leads to different roles, different qualifications, and different services. Perhaps the term library should never have been used in schools. The term resource centre at least establishes bonds with the teaching program, and allows the possibility of the facility being seen as a learning laboratory for youngsters to apply skills for using information effectively, including the use of libraries.

The American Association of School Librarians has not changed its name but for fifteen years has encouraged the term media specialist or library media specialist for school librarians. Isn't this just another barrier? Other teachers in specialist areas (special education, enrichment, computers) haven't come up with fancy new names—they maintain a pride of identity with teaching. "Teacher-librarian" or "learning resource teacher," while not perfect, at least indicate a teaching function and help to break down stereotypes.

Common bonds and links with colleagues will be critical in the development of strong integrated programs. Unnecessary jargon simply confuses and alienates even the most sympathetic of users.

Plan and Target: Assess and Measure
Public Relations Ideas That Work

Kathy Fritts

"Fundamental to the malaise from which conventional school libraries suffer is the universal assumption that students will use them because they are there.... Regarding the library as something less than an irresistible attraction to students is a useful first step in revitalizing it."
•*Hooked On Books*, Daniel Fader

These words are disconcerting. To those of us in the business, libraries, books, and reading are a *pleasure*, but this is simply not so for the vast majority of our students. They have other preoccupations: the Friday night dance; the mad rush of hormones surging through their bodies; getting along with Mom. The school resource center is way down on their list of priorities, and that means that we can never assume that kids know, much less care, what we have to offer. This points to a strong need for program advocacy—we have to go to them, since they won't come to us.

It is not enough any more to have a good program—teacher-librarians need to promote their services aggressively. What follows is a brief checklist to help to determine how you are doing in the promotion end of the business.

PLAN AND TARGET

The crucial part of promotion is settling on a goal. If teacher-librarians don't know where they're going, they're sure to end up somewhere else, or worse yet, exactly where they started. The other side of the coin of goal-setting is targeting an audience. Advertisers take great care to pinpoint their intended audiences, for two reasons; the rifle approach is more effective, and goals change depending on which audience is intended.

- Have a plan, write it out, and follow it. Keep this plan someplace visible, someplace hard to ignore.

- Don't go beyond three or four goals, or effectiveness will be dissipated.

- In goal-setting, be careful not to get bogged down in managerial matters which relate only indirectly to increasing use. (Moving the reference shelving may be very beneficial to usage in the long run, but a more helpful goal in terms of program advocacy might be something like "average at least one booktalk per day.")

- Identify and target a particular audience on which to concentrate, e.g., romance readers, the science department, TAG kids.

- Start with the audience most likely to show a big gain in usage. And remember the rule of 80/20. Sales people always bear in mind that 80 percent of their business comes from 20 percent of their customers. Generally speaking, the same is true in libraries.

- Sit down and write out a cold-blooded, even cynical, analysis of what each potential group of users really wants. If all the principal wants is a quick peek at the sports page daily and a handy sampler of anecdotes for his speeches to the PTA, serve that need. Brainstorm all the groups and subgroups in the school and community; it is surprising how many there are and how different their needs.

ASSESS AND MEASURE

Libraries are very much like small businesses; we provide services, we build a clientele, we promote our wares. But this analogy breaks down when one considers profit and loss, which a small business owner never forgets, and teacher-librarians often ignore.

- Survey a small but random sample of potential patrons at least once a year. Just be sure that the sample really is random and include all major groups.

- Administer a formal survey to staff at least once every two years.

- Do not dream of putting a goal in the plan without a concrete way to measure it. Know in advance exactly how to measure success or failure.

- Keep enough daily records to measure successes objectively, and also to impress administrators and parents, many of whom believe that numbers lend validity to a program.

- Remember that it is not necessary to keep masses of data; frequently a small sampling before and after a promotion effort is plenty.

- Cherish complaints because they give priceless guidance on how to improve service and reach more users even better; compliments are nice but they generally don't help to improve service.

COMMUNICATE VISUALLY

Few of us are graphic artists, merchandising experts, architects, or copywriters; yet somehow we must borrow the skills of these people to give the resource center a clean, inviting, up-to-date look. The old stereotype of the dumpy, frumpy, dreary library had a certain basis in fact, but the resource center doesn't need to look like that if one pays attention to appearance.

- Smile a lot and remind your co-workers to look happy.

- Look well-groomed and professional, even a bit stylish. One high school teacher-librarian wears a Gumby watch, a gift from her 5th grade son. That little touch has done a great deal to win her a friendly reception from students.

- Be seen often at activities outside of school, maybe even sponsor a club or group or coach a sport. It shows concern for what is so important for the kids.

- Have a complete stranger give an honest appraisal of the "first impression." Is the resource center warm, attractive, inviting, easy to use? Are there plants, touches of whimsy, dashes of humor, signs of life, obvious care for the needs of the user? Or does it look institutional and disorganized?

- Visitors new to the building should have no trouble finding the resource center by following the signs.

- The sign system looks professional, consistent throughout, and easy to read. There are almost as many signs as at a supermarket, since people hate to ask directions.

- The entranceway is inviting, uncluttered, and well-lit.

- The checkout area doesn't look like a flea market.

- The floor plan and traffic flow are logical and easy to follow. Areas are clearly marked, and similar areas are close to each other.

- The paint job is bright and clean, and the floor is carpeted.

- The staff wear professionally-done name tags.

- Your publications all use a common logo and the same color paper. The artwork looks clean, sharp, and as professional as possible.

- Keep an idea file for graphic and display possibilities. Have no hesitation about swiping good ideas from others.

- Never hand letter signs, unless you are an expert calligrapher or a professional sign-maker.

- Layouts for publications use the K.I.S.S. principle (keep it simple, stupid), plus judicious use of white space to increase impact.

- Displays take a long time to think up and assemble, so devise some system of saving and organizing the old ones; don't reinvent the wheel. Remember that department stores never let their displays stay up beyond three or four weeks, as they become invisible after a time.

- Use merchandising tricks to increase circulation and impulse borrowing:

    ☐ Face out as many books as possible;

    ☐ Have a paperback or recreational reading display as near the checkout desk as you can. Grocery stores do it with the *National Enquirer*; follow their example;

    ☐ Buy almost all fiction in paperback, since kids like them better;

    ☐ Weed the collection mercilessly—it's a resource center, not a depository;

    ☐ Tend to the seedy-looking books with new Mylar covers and some TLC;

    ☐ Experiment. E.g., try leaving a heap of new books on a table and see what happens to checkout.

COMMUNICATE VERBALLY

Words, both written and spoken, are a teacher-librarian's stock in trade. A few simple reminders can help make these words more effective for program advocacy. If these suggestions seem finicky or too ordinary to bear repeating, remember that it's the little things that make a difference in building a clientele, and that is exactly what we are trying to do.

- Know the name of every kid in school and keep working at it conscientiously. Nothing works more magic in making a young person feel welcome or preventing discipline problems than knowing that student's name.

- Spend a certain amount of time just visiting with kids and staff. It makes for a more relaxed and hospitable atmosphere.

- Never say "Look it up in the card catalog;" get up with a smile and help find what's needed.

- Advertise services outside the resource center, in unexpected places; by the drinking fountain, in the cafeteria, on the PA system.

- Do regular, brief booktalks in classrooms.

- Produce a regular newsletter for staff, and include humor and lots of graphics.

- Gather together an annual report for administrators and use it as the basis for a face-to-face conference.

- Do a regular column in the school paper and use your standard logo.

- Tune into the latest kid craze for a "hook" to hang promotion efforts.

- Gather an advisory committee of staff and students to give you feedback, support, and suggestions. Chosen and nurtured properly, an advisory committee can be priceless.

- Always contribute to the bulk mailings that go home to parents.

- Always give credit to the resource center, in writing and logo, whenever you produce anything anywhere for anybody, i.e. faculty slide show, bookmarks, whatever. Where not enough people know what a resource center or media center is, be careful to use "library" instead.

- Whenever something special happens in the resource center, invitations and notices go to school board members and administrators.

- Be the "book person" in the school and make constant efforts to keep teachers reminded of new books in their area of interest, articles they might like to read, reviews of books to order.

- Write and publish lots of short handouts for kids to keep or take home—lists for vacation reading; public library hours; research hints; bibliographies of all kinds (snappily illustrated); bookmarks; suggestions to parents. Make sure that they are plainly marked "resource center" or "library," and have the logo and standard color.

PROGRAMMING

For some teacher-librarians, program advocacy means "programming." However, we need a wider perspective on the problem of programming. It's a problem because, quite simply, library programs do not make readers. They may be lots of fun, and people may feel more positive towards the facility, but programming takes up a tremendous amount of time and may have only a peripheral effect on the main goal, which is to connect books and readers.

This does not mean we should abandon programming. It just means that we should keep our goals clearly in mind and make sure that programming will help us achieve those goals. For instance, if our budget is anemic and no amount of real service to our clientele has improved it, perhaps a fabulous, time-consuming, splashy program which will make the front page of the local paper is just the lever you need to pry more money from the School Board. In weighing a library program, return to the first steps in program advocacy: plan and target, assess and measure.

- If a program takes too much time and effort for the projected gains, drop it or don't repeat it.

- Save time and increase impact by utilizing tradition in programming, i.e. certain events "belong" to the resource center.

- Showcase the work of others and publicize these displays thoroughly. It provides quick and easy programming and creates much good will.

- Sponsor lots of little contests and events which are quick to arrange.

- Don't reward wrongdoing by having an amnesty if you charge fines! Instead, hold raffles with tickets going to those without fines. Amnesty for fines sends the entirely wrong message.

- Latch onto someone else's program by having the event in the resource center and doing some of the legwork. If it's in the resource center, the teacher-librarian gets some of the halo effect without so much work.

- Use gimmicks and little rewards to encourage your heavy users (remember the 80/20 rule?).

Program advocacy may seem like just one more duty heaped on an overworked teacher-librarian. However, if we do not get the message out to our clientele, they will not come and beg for our services. Without program advocacy, indifference is the best we can hope for; disaster in the form of budget cuts, personnel reductions or censorship is more likely.

Marketing Services for Young Adults in the School Library

Carol Hauser

When I began to consider the implications of the word "marketing," I realized that it was a term I had long associated with the world of business—not education.

A trip to the reference shelves soon clarified the term for me, gave me some structure for what I plan to say here—and made me realize that my operation is more closely akin to the business world than I had imagined. My research told me that marketing is "the planning and implementation of a strategy for the distribution of a product or service." It begins with research into consumer needs and attitudes, assessment of competitors' products and involves advertising and promotion. Marketing plans form an important strategy for new products and expansion. The broad scope of this definition made me more comfortable about sharing what I feel is germane to meeting the needs of today's young adult, and my concern for the young people I meet in that small segment of their world that I share with them.

Because of its very location, the school library, in setting goals and objectives and planning its program and services, must be involved in comprehensive and ongoing needs assessment in many areas. Our prime function is support of the curriculum and academic programs and thus, many of the student needs we address are those ascribed to the student by the curriculum through the expectations inherent in each discipline. Students as library users in the academic program require up-to-date, relevant, readable material; instruction in the identification, retrieval and utilization of information; and practice in organizing, presenting and sharing this information in a variety of ways. As schools also take as their goal the broad education of the student, their need for cultural enrichment, positive attitudes to self, and realization of the need for life-long learning are recognized. In pursuit of these goals, we must consider each young adult as an individual, with a broad range of personal interests reflected in the demands they bring into the library. The school library must be in touch with the interests of the student population and develop a collection at once specific to the curriculum, yet broad enough to meet the more personal student needs.

Integral to this needs assessment should be an awareness of other information sources available to the student and the many influences in their lives. Proximity of a public library, availability and use of books, magazines and television in the home are part of the profile of a student population—a profile that changes with each yearly change in student population.

Within the context of a school program, positive interaction with the administration and the teaching staff is crucial for the development of a meaningful library program, and consistent library access and use by the young adult. Administrators are responsible for finances, timetabling and a school philosophy. All of these can very successfully impede or contribute to the growth of a school library program. The

scheduling of several reading periods into a weekly timetable can bring every student into the library over a two- or three-week period. Naturally, this makes a profound difference in a student's interest in materials that are available. Such a simple timetabling move increases significantly our interaction with these young adults—and their requests and demands make continual collection development even more integral to our services to them.

In situations where administrators do not perceive library-based activity as valid, only the most confident teacher will continue to provide student access to the library. It is, however, through the classroom teacher that we can most successfully gain access to students. The ultimate goal is constant communication between teacher and teacher-librarian, and the resultant frequent use of the library materials and services to support the academic program through co-operative planning, teaching and evaluating a unit of study. However, reality frequently falls short of this ideal. There are as many different levels of teacher-librarian interaction, and varieties of library use, as there are teachers. The teacher-librarian frequently has to be quite devious in her efforts to draw young people into the library, by means of interaction with the teaching staff. We must be constantly alert to the smallest opportunity for integrating library use into the program. Where opportunity presents itself, the teacher-librarian should be positive, assertive and specific about the materials and services that can be provided for the teacher and students.

Displays, presentations and workshops during staff meetings and professional development days can alert staff members to materials available and ways of utilizing facilities. Distributing a list of subject-related skills that can best be developed in a library setting may encourage a teacher to use the facility. If a teacher remains uncomfortable with library use, informing her of materials she may expect her students to use in independent assignments will draw in students looking for help. When teachers assist in the selection of materials purchased, and these are circulated to departments before general circulation, students are more frequently sent to look for specific titles.

Integration of library use and library-based skills into the academic area is the ideal. But integration need not begin specifically with the academic areas. In my first year at my present school, the principal insisted on greater use of the library by the language arts teachers. At the same time, Grade 7 language arts teachers wished to bring students in on a weekly basis for a "library-based" lesson. Pleased at having access to the students, but wishing to make the lessons meaningful, I kept in constant touch with teachers in all other subject areas, and correlated the skills developed with classroom activities in the academic areas. Most lessons were prefaced by telling students about an assignment that was approaching in which the skill could be applied. All teachers received frequent communications regarding skills covered, and what could be expected from the Grade 7 students they taught. They soon became interested in how this could be related in grades 8 and 9 classes—and we were away!

Student teachers, when made aware of the potential of the library and the consultative services available, have been very effective in integrating library use into their program. Parental attitudes to the school library can be instrumental in encouraging library use. Communications with parents through the school newsletter, and displays and invitations to browse in the library during parent-teacher interviews, alerts parents to program and facility. When the teacher-librarian is available for joint consultation at such interviews, more than one student has become a regular library user through encouragement from all three parties.

I feel very strongly that the library, aside from its role in support of the academic program, has a life of its own and can provide valuable services for the young adult who does not utilize it academically. Such students are frequently the most difficult to reach, to draw in, and to convince that the library has something for them. As I tell them, "It's here—it's for you—it's free. You just have to bring materials back."

Our library hours are designed to accommodate students who are dropped off at the school by parents on the way to work. As many of our students take the bus, few stay after school. Thus we remain open at noon hour, and at this time the library is used in its broadest sense for homework, research, recreational reading, audio-visual viewing, listening and production work. We have invested in numerous tape recorders and headphones and have attempted to develop a listening library. Periodicals are very popular at this time, and when ordering I invite recommendations from students and accommodate them where possible. Noon hour is an invaluable time for me to informally circulate, to talk to students, and to recommend recreational reading.

Most of the activities designed to draw the young adult into the library tend not to be of the "major celebration" nature. They are features and activities that evolve from, and tie into, the mainstream activities of the school and the teenagers' own lives, and hopefully celebrate on a daily basis what it is to be young and discovering the world. We do have special events, however, and our one major celebration is a film week designed to introduce students to adaptations of print to other media. Students eat their lunches while short adaptations of films based on young adult novels are screened. These films are available from the National Film Board and our own Media Services of the Calgary Board of Education. I try to vary the films from year to year, but choices are always made with boys in mind, for they constitute 70 to 80 percent of our "casual clientele." On the last day, students vote for their favorite film and a draw is made for show passes and paperback versions of the titles screened.

A close liaison with other departments in the school brings to light activities that translate well to a library setting. Our own version of Lunchbox Theatre is created when students bring their lunches and are entertained with readers' theatre or a make-up workshop put on by the drama department. Lawn chairs being made by students in the woodworking shop for a school raffle were brought in for students to use while reading. A quilting loom, featuring a student project, was set up in one corner of the library and soon became a center of interest as groups of students worked on the quilt. In conjunction with the Language Arts Department, creative writing contests—prose and poetry—are held in the library each year. The best pieces of work are typed and bound in a book that is housed in the 800s and circulates regularly.

As a result of a lesson to a home economics class on reading and storytelling to the very young, we have developed a small collection of paperback books for teenagers to use when babysitting.

At the beginning of each year, I use a fast-paced slide/tape presentation for Grades 8 and 9 to review library facilities and services. I maintain a core set of slides but each spring I photograph Grades 7 and 8 students involved in various activities in the library, and incorporate these into the production. Just one class has to see the production, and the word spreads. Students are eager to see themselves and their friends on the screen!

The search for good recreational reading is aided by student interest. In developing this aspect of our collection, I encourage recommendations by students, and consider them when purchasing. The range of interests at this level is very broad, but it is possible to target the rise and fall of trends. The creation of colorful centres housing computer or fantasy books provides easy access to these, as well as a common ground for meeting other students of like interests.

We often process new books in the library proper so that students can see what will be available shortly. There is nothing quite like the lure of a book "not yet available for circulation" to quicken the pulses of students and give them cause to return the next day. These are but a few of the strategies we have employed to make students aware of the potential of their library. They may have been successful yesterday and today—but tomorrow?—well that's another matter.

According to my research, marketing plans form an important strategy for new products and expansion—in short, for change; and if any single word characterizes today's world for the young adult, it surely is change—external changes in the world around and the powerful physical and internal changes of maturation. Librarians must keep in touch with these changes and be sensitive and responsive to implications for program and services. We must be aware that while what we often see is an adult, what we are hearing and must listen to is *youth*—youth that requires guidance, instruction and direction.

"Saying Farewell to Miss Prune Face"; or, Marketing School Library Services

Pat Cavill

Nothing irks me more than being at a conference workshop session and hearing the speaker, an "expert" from another field, say "Well, I don't know much about libraries. I don't have time to read, but...." I always say to myself (and to anyone else who will listen!) "Well, if he doesn't know a thing about libraries, why is he here and why am I here? And why didn't he find something out about libraries beforehand—do a little market research on his target audience?" At that point, I either tune out or walk out.

Well, here I am, a dyed-in-the-wool public library person, writing on marketing the school library resource center, and I feel like taking a deep breath and saying, "Well, I don't know much about school libraries, but...."

The truth is simply that I've never *worked* in a school resource centre, but I do have opinions and feelings about them. These emotions come from being a kid, being a teenager, being an adult and becoming a librarian. I have made several observations about school libraries arising from 17 years of advocating school-public library cooperation in a regional library setting and, most recently, from having eight school-housed public libraries under my jurisdiction.

So perhaps my view from the periphery is one which allows me some objectivity: my impressions are not based on a familiarity that allows things to go unseen.

To begin with, then, let me share with you some experiences from which I have obviously drawn some conclusions. Going from the specific to the general and back to the specific again will allow me to share some communication theory which should be helpful in any situation.

I don't remember much about my school library prior to high school. But my high school librarian was, and I do not exaggerate, the worst possible combination of the stereotypical teacher-librarian, complete with bun and rimless glasses. I did not grow up dreaming of being a librarian some day as a result of her influence on my life. Instead, for my three years in high school I worked in the school "bookstore," noon hours and after school. This consisted of a couple of locking, moveable display cases full of paperbacks supplied by a paperback wholesaler. I made 5 percent on every book sold. Before too long I was doing mini-book reviews briefly on the school intercom once a week; I featured particular titles on posters throughout the school; I ran contests and convinced all the English teachers to order their class sets of Shakespeare through me at the bookstore. I can assure you that all this was a lot more fun than being a member of the library assistants' club under Miss Prune Face, (which is what we called her!).

Potential Lifelong Conclusion #1: **school libraries are not fun.**

An acquaintance of mine, on finding out that I was a librarian, said that he hadn't used a library since high school.

Libraries gave him "bad vibes" he said. It turned out that in his rural high school, the library was where kids were sent for detention.

Potential Lifelong Conclusion #2: **libraries are a form of punishment.**

I was awaiting my turn to speak to the teaching staff of an elementary school, wanting to explain to them first hand what the public library could and could not provide to students. I had a copy of the staff meeting agenda in my hand. I was interested in hearing item number 6, Librarian's Report. The librarian did not lift her face from the papers on her knees and mumbled "I've got some new publisher's catalogues. I'll be routing them to everyone. I want your orders in by the end of June." End of Report.

Potential Lifelong Conclusion #3: **"school librarians don't get no respect." And nor should they.**

A school-housed public library has recently moved to a new location in an addition to the school. The librarian was "told" she was moving and was not once consulted in the process. She has ended up with a too-small library (smaller than the classroom she previously occupied) with a mezzanine. The latter has been the bane of her existence.

Potential Lifelong Conclusion #4: **school librarians aren't important.**

A well-intentioned school library "consultant" is putting in hundreds of hours of volunteer and staff time re-cataloguing all the public library collection in a school-housed public library. The fact that the public library collection is professionally catalogued and on a microfiche catalogue at her elbow is irrelevant. She wants cards in the card catalogue.

Potential Lifelong Conclusion #5: **school libraries are dreary, dull places because of no natural light.**

Another school-housed public library needed more shelving in the classroom that was being used for the library. Over the summer holidays, when the library staff were away, the school district carpenters built new shelving and installed it in front of all the classroom windows (the only place that they could see to put the stuff).

Potential Lifelong Conclusion #6: **school librarians drive me crazy!**

Now to give equal time to public libraries for purposes of illustration, let me offer the following analogy:

One of the biggest frustrations most librarians face is that the people on funding bodies aren't library users. This includes aldermen, town councillors, trustees, legislators—the whole lot.

Any marketing plan that a library implements is going to have a strategy for reading these decision-makers and turning them into fanatic library supporters. They are a prime target group.

Let's assume then, that a city alderman has finally received the library's message. At age 59 he decides to walk the block and a half from city hall to the main library and take out his very first public library card. His first impressions of the library include any of the following:

- a band of closed-circuit TV screens with too many different messages about what's happening in the library, none of which tells him what he's looking for—where to get a library card.

- large directional signs informing him that the 100s are to the left, the 700s are on the third floor, that acquisitions and cataloging are on the fifth floor but he's not allowed to go there—signs that show that this is a complex institution and he needs help to find his way around.

- a desk that says "information" but the first person he sees is a security guard.

- signs saying all the things you cannot do in the library: you can't eat, drink or smoke; you can't keep your books for longer than three weeks; you need two pieces of identification to get a library card; a list of fines.

- the first person he encounters could be the union shop steward who is hostile the day after a particularly frustrating union meeting, or a person who has just decided to apply for another job because he/she is dissatisfied with the library's working conditions.

- a fresh and eager young reference librarian wearing blue jeans.

- a person at a desk who is not yet aware of a policy change that the library board and council know about.

- the material he wants is in circulation.

- the material he wants is missing, or not where it should be.

So it would not be surprising to find out that the alderman feels he's been "had" by false advertising, and now there's a public library somewhere that could be in trouble!

What I have been talking about is a series of "first impressions," ranging from my own, through to those of children in school resource centres, to those of people whose support is critical to the survival of an institution. The problem with all the examples cited is that, for the most part, libraries, both school and public, are being judged unfairly. Conclusions are being made based on inadequate information. But *most* conclusions are based on inadequate information. Does something like this sound familiar?

"The Hotel St. Audrey? Oh no, I wouldn't stay there if I were you. The service is lousy. No, I've never been in the rooms, but the restaurant is dreadful." Yes indeed, the impression you get of a hotel is not formed by the grandeur of the rooms, but by the way you were treated at the registration desk, in the lounge, or in the restaurant. And these first impressions are the ones that stay with people.

If you accept the fact that first impressions do count, you have got to make sure that you as a person, and your resource center make the best possible use of the small amount of time you have to make that impression. This leads us right to the subject of "image."

I won't bore or offend you again by repeating the stereotype of librarians anywhere. We only have to talk to a few people outside our profession to know that the stereotype is alive and well in the minds of many people. And we only have to look at the stereotypes in our own minds of such persons as the used car salesman, the accountant, the advertising executive and so on, to realize how deeply these stereotypes can be entrenched in even the most rational mind. So what does this stereotype have to do with the image of the institutions we represent, you may ask. Absolutely everything! And individually and collectively, we have to do something about that image. Personally I would much rather be judged by the IBM stereotype—a smart, efficient, competent, successful, and yes, perhaps even slick and uncaring person—than that other that gets me called Miss Prune Face behind my back!

I suggest that the first step in changing the resource center's image is define what you want it to be. This is much easier when program goals and objectives are communicated at all levels; where there is a common sense of purpose and direction. The teacher-librarian is indeed at the mercy of the school administration in that regard.

Remember all those horrible stories that I told at the beginning? Not one of those situations had a professional teacher-librarian in the resource center. You don't have to *be* a professional in order to have a professional attitude, but those particularly nasty examples *do* reflect on your profession as teachers and teacher-librarians. In the same fashion, public librarians are judged by the clericals staffing the circulation desk. To the patrons, all library staff everywhere are "librarians." How much training you have or don't have is completely irrelevant to the patron. I don't care if the person putting gas in my car is a student working part time or the owner of the garage. Just give me what I want and don't bother me with the details!

I am mentioning staff now because they play a major role in presenting the library's image. Spirit needs to be built into staff and volunteers because enthusiasm is contagious. Little things mean a lot. Keeping the staff informed and up to date makes them feel that they are important to the library, and this is always accomplished best by one on one conversation. Soliciting the input of staff and using it makes them feel they have a commitment, a stake in the library.

Staff relations are one example of how to create a better image. The visual impact of the library, whether or not it's neat (I believe that comfortable "clutter" is fine in your own living room, but is not appropriate for a library), whether or not it is properly equipped, furnished and maintained are critical factors in determining image. Please don't forget adequate signage. But the contributing factor most often overlooked is the merchandising of the collection itself. Yes, keep the books in good repair; yes, have lots of displays; but most important, weed. What earthly use does a yearbook from 1985 all the way back to 1957 have to high school students? Old encyclopedias? (I've seen them in many resource centers.)

One of my favorite stories comes from a merchandising seminar I went to, sponsored by our local Chamber of Commerce. The seminar leader, a "down home" sort from Georgia (note the "stereotype!") asked if there was someone in the audience who had a women's clothing store. The owner of "Marlene's Place" nodded expectantly. "Has anyone," the seminar leader said quietly and thoughtfully, "Has anyone ever come into your store and asked to see your collection of sleeves?" "No!", Marlene laughed. "Then why the hell do you display your clothing with only the sleeves showing?" he yelled at her. Marlene loved it; I loved it. No one wants to see your collection of book spines either! Thousands of dollars go into book cover design, so take advantage of it! Weed the collection, make room on the shelves and "sell" the best you've got.

If cleaning up your own back yard, or creating a positive and consistent image for your resource center is the first step, then promoting this image throughout the school, the school district, to parents, to your professional association and so on is next on the list.

You are confident that you can and are doing the best possible job as a teacher-librarian in integrating the resource centre with the school's program and curriculum. But, I think, in even the best-funded resource center scenarios the possibilities always exists that funding can be cut back in order to buy basketballs. No teacher-librarian can rest on laurels for very long, particularly in circumstances that have turned education funding into an economic cat fight. So what can the teacher-librarian do to ensure that the resource center's message will be heard loud and clear by decision-makers throughout the system?

COMMUNICATION

In the same way that you have only a short time to make a first impression, your message only has a short time to register in the mind of a school administrator who is bombarded daily with all kinds of messages. So you may feel you have communicated your intent, because you wrote a memo, made a telephone call, called a meeting. If the required action didn't occur, it's not your fault. Isn't it? Before any communication can occur, you must be aware of barriers to communication. They fall into four broad areas: physical, semantic, personal and environmental.

What are the physical barriers to communication? Distance, noise, time, distractions, space. Let's go back to our alderman. He could have encountered a physical barrier to communication that prevented him from pursuing his quest for a library card. The closed circuit televisions and the directional signage could have been confusing and distracting. The very size of the place could have been intimidating. He may have gone into information overload the minute he walked in

the front door. If he turned around and walked out, the library did not communicate with this person, even though it thought it did. Shelves placed over the windows in the resource center I mentioned could be a physical barrier because they create an unpleasant environment, not the least bit conducive to communication.

Semantic barriers are ones that libraries put up all over the place. What do the words 'reference,' 'bibliography,' 'computer search' mean to someone who has never used a library before? Do you know what pictures the word 'book truck' conjures up in the mind of a non-library user? "It's on that truck over there." The person doesn't see what they think is a truck, so the communication doesn't occur. When I applied for my first job in a library back in 1969 as a student assistant, I was asked if I wanted to work in circulation or stacks. I had a pretty good idea what circulation was, but no idea what stacks were. So I said "stacks" and doomed myself to three years hard labor shelving the PS-PZ collection on the third floor of the university's main library.

The absolutely worst offender in jargon is the Dewey Decimal System itself. Think of the person who has learned, to her amazement, that the library has cookbooks. She decides to go into the public library to look for a new cheesecake recipe. How is she to know that second floor, 600-Applied Science, is where she wants to go? Does "600" in large numerals at the end of a bookstack explain to a school kid that this is where to find the pet books?

Even the word "patron" can be confusing. A sign saying "patron registration" could, to some people, mean where you make charitable donations, as in a patron of the symphony or the theater.

When you combine library jargon with teaching jargon, you end up with "LRC" instead of library! It may be obvious to you, but it sure wasn't to me when I first heard the term. Ask some of your students what some of your library jargon means. The responses, albeit amusing, will be quite an eyeopener.

Personal barriers to communication are the most difficult with which to deal. These include all the attitudes, beliefs, values, opinions and stereotypes that a person holds dear. Supposing, for example, the principal of your school used to work at that elementary school which had the wimpy "librarian" handing out publishers' catalogs. If this principal were a 50 year old male, he would not likely have had the opportunity to have ever seen a good resource center in a school. If his only experience with a library was that one, then what could he possibly know about the value of professional book selection?

Suppose that I hadn't gone away to library school and was left instead with one of those "Potential Lifelong Conclusions" and ingrained stereotypes? Attitudes don't change overnight, so there is always a formidable personal barrier to communication for you to overcome.

Some people are intimidated by new technology. A person's fear of using a microfiche catalog and the automated circulation system might be a barrier.

Environmental barriers are those that arise from political, social or economic differences of perspective. Management/union negotiations are a good example of an environmental barrier. How much effective communication is going to happen when there's a physical barrier of a table, a semantic barrier of jargon, personal barriers that include stereotypes of union and management alike, and the environmental barrier of totally different backgrounds and perspectives on the issues at hand? How much effective communication can possibly occur during a long teacher strike?

Marketing your resource center's services then means a number of complex and intertwined activities.

- Clean up your own backyard and develop an image with which you are comfortable.

- Identify the individuals or organizations whose support is critical to your library's operation. These become your target groups. Your most important target group is usually the smallest, and you will be surprised to realize that your most important target group is likely your school principal and not the students you serve daily. Other target groups that you may identify, depending on your circumstances, might be the teachers (group these by their common traits; for example, English teachers, physical education teachers, etc.), parent advisory groups, local or provincial/state library and teachers' associations. What you are doing here is getting intensely political. You are asking yourself "which of all my target groups are most important to me and my library? Whom do I most need on my side?"

- For each target group find a product or service that would be of particular interest. Maybe you spotted a bibliography on coaching skills for various sports. Photocopy it, send it to the gym teacher, with a personal note attached. Know the wants and needs of your important target groups and constantly be on the lookout for information that is relevant to their personal and professional needs (market research!). Watch for TV and newspaper advertising and see how cleverly it matches the product to the target group. (No, sorry, those wonderful Michael J. Fox Pepsi ads are not targeted at us. We're the "old Pepsi generation" and we've been replaced by a new one!).

You really can learn a lot by being aware of marketing done by business. For example, the new Coke was an unmitigated failure, resulting in bringing back the old Coke as Coke Classic. Company executives made a huge error and I'm sure some heads rolled as a result of poor market testing.

- Regularly evaluate results. Watch for feedback. Did the principal stop by to thank you for clipping out that book review on west coast landscaping? Did the music teacher order a personal copy of *Guide to the Best Classical Music on Compact Disc* after you'd pointed out its existence? Does the art teacher now volunteer time to professionally design your booklists because you've been fulfilling her information needs? You have to make yourself indispensable to your major target groups.

Marketing the library means reaching out beyond the walls in the fashion described because you know that information is power. And you need power in order to continue to build the credibility of your profession; in order to continue to improve services and in order to bring resource centers into the mainstream of education rather than as an easily ignored adjunct.

As educators, you are preparing people for life-long learning. You know the value of both formal and informal education. So why don't you teach yourself more about human behavior and communication; read about how the world's greatest car salesman made his money, and attend workshops on the subjects of marketing and merchandising?

I have a selfish reason for requesting this because as a public librarian, I get the students after school and on weekends! I have always believed that good public library service and good school library service go hand in hand. I want kids that come through the school system to remain readers and users of public libraries, so I want strong school resource centers. Change your image, sell your wares and please continue the fight for teacher-librarians in all school libraries.

7 Steps to Developing Support from School Principals

Ken Haycock

1. **Plan a Strategy**—Full information is crucial. Does the principal know and understand the role of the school library as fundamental to learning, as much an approach to teaching as a place in the school? Where would this knowledge come from? Certainly not the training institutions or professional literature and rarely from the school district. It is equally important

to observe the communication link and patterns within the school to determine who is most important in communicating with the administration and why this is so.

2. **Confer Regularly**—Every teacher-librarian should meet on a regular basis in planned meetings with the

school principal. This is essential for ensuring that time is available for communication, that the administrator is involved in program appraisal and improvement and that it becomes an important part of administrative routine.

3. **Communicate Effectively** — Avoid library jargon and discuss goals and directions in the common language of education. What are your short and long range objectives? What is it specifically that you would like to accomplish this month, this year, this term? The library will not be perceived as an essential component of the school program unless it is viewed as integral to both the teaching and learning taking place in the school.

4. **Be Specific** — What are the areas requiring attention? Be specific in your request and be sure to include the benefits that will accrue directly to the school program. Translate your budget into program terms. How much money is required to purchase book and non-book materials for that particular unit which you plan to team teach with a classroom teacher so that there are sufficient materials for the students involved? Providing an adequate number and range of materials is essential to the success of the program.

5. **Be Professional** — Involve the principal in the definition of priorities but you have to make final decisions as to what will be done for that particular group of students and teachers in your particular situation. Recognize your integrity and exercise your professional judgement.

6. **Involve the Administrator** — Does the principal understand the function of the resource centre and the role of the teacher-librarian? Have you discussed your role in cooperative program planning and teaching and the varying successes with different subject areas and grade levels? Has the administrator been encouraged to question prospective new teachers as to how they might involve the teacher-librarian in their program and question teachers currently on staff as to how they are using the resource centre and its services in their teaching program?

7. **Be Visible** — Make sure that the resource centre is on the agenda for staff or department meetings, and that there are displays in the staff room about services as well as new materials. Attention should be paid to displays and bulletin boards outside of the resource centre as much as inside (who would put a 'for sale' sign in their living room rather than on their front lawn?). Be involved with your teaching colleagues and display yourself and your services without the undue humility and modesty so characteristic of the profession.

Effective communication is the key to development of successful school library programs. The administrator plays an important role in establishing an environment for growth and the development of important services. It should be recognized that school administrators often do not have as much background, information, and experience with teacher-librarians as is desirable. The future might very well rest with teacher-librarians who ensure that teachers on school staffs become knowledgeable and experienced in planning and developing units of instruction with them using team teaching as an effective method of integrating research and study skills in their programs. As long as we are willing only to react to teacher requests rather than initiate cooperative programs, we are going to continue to have teachers without any knowledge of school library services promoted to positions of responsibility and then wonder why we do not get the level of support that we require from these same administrators.

Pyramid Power:
The Teacher-Librarian and Censorship

Larry Amey

No librarian is more vulnerable to censorship attacks than a school librarian. There are reasons for this and they are best appreciated by comparing the school library and the public library. The public library is fairly well understood as a place that holds all sorts of materials for all sorts of readers — children, teenagers and adults. This broad mandate gives the public library some degree of protection. Moreover, many public libraries have strengthened their position by adopting an open access policy. Open access makes all materials in the library available to everyone regardless of age. This means that the library staff do not prevent patrons from choosing and borrowing any materials which they desire. Such a policy declares that librarians will not assume parental responsibility for a child's selection and use of library materials. This burden

I received a call at the library school from a high school librarian sounding very upset. "Have you heard about the censorship problem here?" she demanded. "I may lose my job over this!"

When she managed to catch her breath, the teacher-librarian described her problem. Apparently, the local fundamentalist preacher and his wife had paid a visit to her library, and had searched through a large number of books, carefully noting "bad" words. They subsequently typed a list of these words on a long sheet, and on the following Sunday, stood outside the church, distributing a copy to each church member. At the top of the sheet was the heading: THIS IS THE SORT OF FILTH IN OUR SCHOOL LIBRARY!

The librarian said, with fear in her voice, "They may even get an interview with the Minister of Education over this! What am I going to do?" I asked the obvious question: "Do you have a collection policy?" "No," she responded, "I'm afraid we haven't."

On learning that the library had no collection policy, I knew that support would have to be sought elsewhere. I contacted the school library association. They indicated that they were aware of the problem, but felt that nothing much could be done about it as their next scheduled meeting was in two months' time.

I turned to the teachers' union (of which all teacher-librarians are members). The response was guarded. They hadn't heard about any problem with censorship. I suggested that they might want to consider a statement of support—something declaring that the union stood behind the library and supports the principle of intellectual freedom. "Not all of our members would agree with that," was all she said in reply.

Things began to look very bleak.

The preacher and his wife were successful in gaining an appointment with the Minister of Education. The newspapers took up the subject, and the letters began to hum. As a last resort I called the provincial writers' federation.

The writers' federation knew all about the problem. Among the books being attacked were some works by their members. They were mad about it, and they were prepared to help. Very soon, letters—concise, well-written letters— began to appear in the newspapers. They were written by well-known writers, poets, teachers and other respected, influential people. They spoke out against censorship, and they defended the school library.

The action that truly turned the tide occurred, however, when one of their most prominent members, and one of the country's outstanding fiction writers, was awarded an honorary doctorate by a university in the same area as the high school library. He chose intellectual freedom as the topic of his speech at the ceremony. This strong, persuasive speech, which commented on the attempt to ban one of his novels at the high school, was widely reported.

In the face of such public declarations, the censors folded their tents and retreated. The librarian emerged bruised but triumphant, and she immediately set about developing a collection policy.

is placed back on the parents, and a parent's signature is often required acknowledging this arrangement before a borrower's card will be issued.

This approach is rather effective in discouraging censorship challenges in the public library, but it cannot be used by the school resource center. Many teacher-librarians are required on being hired, to sign a teacher's contract which contains a clause that specifically requires that all teachers act in *loco parentis*, that is, in the place of parents.

This is generally taken to mean that the teacher-librarian must assume responsibility for all the library materials which the student may borrow and read.

Also, the school resource center, unlike the public library, is seen as specifically intended for the use and instruction of children and young adults, that is, as part of the program of education. There are differing views, however, about the nature of the educational process and the school resource center role in it. Some parents regard education as a process in which young people, like empty vessels, are filled to the brim with good things. The resource center, in this view, should consist solely of exemplary materials. To include books in a school resource center is to endorse and sanctify them, according to this philosophy. The argument that education is a process in which children are taught to think critically for themselves, and that this is best accomplished by exposing them to a wide range of materials, is not warmly embraced in some circles.

Teacher-librarians are also made vulnerable to censorship attacks by their professional isolation. Public librarians generally work as part of a team of professionals who can be turned to for support, understanding, and encouragement in times of trouble. The teacher-librarian, however, is most often the sole library professional in the school, outnumbered by classroom teachers, who may not have thought through the issues concerning the library and intellectual freedom, and the principal, who may prefer to run a quiet ship untroubled by censorship disputes.

This leaves the teacher-librarian in an exposed position, rather like the final block atop a pyramid. Standing alone and unprotected, the teacher-librarian is an easy target, one that can be flicked off the pyramid by the snap of a censor's finger.

How, then, can you protect yourself? This article describes a method to broaden your base of support, to increase your pyramid power, to ensure that you no longer stand alone.

To begin, it is worth considering what you can't do in regard to censorship:

1. **You can't prevent people from wanting to censor.**

Censorship has been a popular pursuit since Adam was outfitted with a fig leaf, and all signs indicate that it will continue. In an excellent study, Jenkinson[6] surveyed the extent of censorship activity in one of Canada's prairie provinces. He examined censorship challenges in school and public libraries in Manitoba. During a two-year period, he found that these libraries were subject to 230 challenges to more than 150 titles. Manitoba is not unique. Another study,[9] limited to public libraries, found that during a one year period, more than one challenge each week took place in an Alberta public library. An examination of newspaper reports makes clear that attacks on library collections occur frequently throughout North America.

2. You can't anticipate what will be censored.

Some teacher-librarians hope to avoid the problem by sagaciously anticipating what the community will object to, and carefully excluding such materials from their purchase lists. It doesn't work. Everything a wise person has said, is potentially censorable by someone, somewhere, some time, for some reason. This seems an extravagant pronouncement until one begins to examine specific examples. Each term, I ask my Collections Management class to select at random a recent issue of the *Newsletter on Intellectual Freedom*[8] and to examine the recent challenges to materials. This invaluable source serves as a barometer of censorship activity. It provides a running bibliography of all published material on intellectual freedom, articles and commentary on key censorship cases, polls of censorship attitudes, and, most usefully, an ongoing register of censorship challenges, entitled "Targets of the Censor." No matter which issue is selected, entries in this register never fail to astound the students. They are amazed by some of the titles attacked, and by the factors that motivate censors. For example, a fairly recent issue[8] included some of the following titles:

The Adventures of Huckleberry Finn
Animal Farm
The Carpetbaggers
The Crucible
Deenie
Forever
George's Marvelous Medicine
Go Ask Alice
The Grapes of Wrath
The Great Gatsby
The Life Cycle of a Chicken
Lord of the Flies
Love Story
My Fair Lady
1984
Scruples
Slaughterhouse Five
To Kill a Mockingbird
Wuthering Heights

I will not review why each of these books was challenged, but one or two examples will serve to illustrate: *Wuthering Heights* was objected to for its supernatural content; *The Crucible*, for witchcraft; *1984* and *My Fair Lady*, for religious reasons; *The Great Gatsby*, for glamorizing adultery; and the Pulitzer Prize winning novel, *To Kill a Mockingbird* (which was on a supplemental reading list for Grade eight) was attacked by black parents and the National Association for the Advancement of Colored People (NAACP)!

These sorts of challenges are not limited to the United States. Jenkinson's study uncovered some remarkable examples in Manitoba. Along with the predictable challenges to anything that Judy Blume has set pen to, there were other targets that might not have been anticipated: *Little Red Riding Hood*; volumes 14 and 15 of the *Childcraft Encyclopedia*; Sendak's *In the Night Kitchen*; Mayer's *There's a Nightmare in My Closet*; Zindel's *The Pigman*; Lee's *Garbage Delight*; and *Mother Goose*! It is, indeed, a strange world in which someone will complain about *Mother Goose* because of morality, obscenity, and violence, *Garbage Delight* because of violence, *In the Night Kitchen* because of nudity and obscenity, and two volumes of the encyclopedia because they include human reproduction.

These dismal examples serve, if nothing else, to illustrate the impossibility of second-guessing the censor and anticipating what will be attacked. The next time you put *The Three Little Pigs* on the shelf, you should be aware that someone may be disturbed by the violence in that cautionary tale; and *Treasure Island* has been known to offend those who claim that the handicapped are demeaned by the way in which that salty old pirate, Long John Silver, is portrayed.

3. You can't develop a foolproof defense, a gardol shield against censorship.

Merle Haggard, in one of his songs, advises: "You can't hide yourself from love. Love will come and find you every time." Censorship is a bit like that. In spite of this, Jenkinson found that some of his respondents were trying to hide. A clerk in an urban K-12 school admitted that "any such books that may cause a challenge to surface, I have taken off the shelf;" a principal of a rural K-12 school asserted that "I have on a number of occasions destroyed books I felt did not reflect the community's nor my own personal taste or values;" a vice-principal in a rural 4 to 8 school could claim that his school had had no complaints in 21 years because, "in my capacity as vice-principal, I try to ensure that books which would cause controversy are never placed in the library." While withholding any comment about the quality of collections built upon such a philosophy, I would observe, nevertheless, that this sort of strategy is self-deceptive ... you can't hide yourself from censorship; censorship will come and find you every time. It may take a little longer in some cases, but when it does, it is apt to be doubly disturbing to the self-satisfied, self-censor.

Let us now consider what you can do:

1. Cheer up!

Remind yourself that you are not encircled by a guerrilla army of censors. Snipers from the political right and left are not in every wheat field, hidden in every orchard, and behind every lobster pot. Only a small minority—albeit a vocal, vociferous, and sometimes well-organized minority—wish to deprive their fellow citizens of their right to read. It is true that these people often pepper the letters to the editor columns of the local newspapers with their intemperate views and librarians, faced with such campaigns, may begin to believe that they represent a great tide of public opinion. This is hardly the case, and we do an injustice to our neighbors by harboring such fears. In general, the public provides strong, if quiet, support for intellectual freedom, and resists those who would censor. A national survey on the subject has not been carried out recently, but it is interesting to note the results of a survey on what is regarded as an even more controversial topic: sex education in the schools. The letter columns in the newspapers dealing with this topic might lead one to conclude that this is a highly charged issue, facing massive public opposition. The Gallup poll showed otherwise: over 83 percent of Canadian adults indicated that they believe that sex education should be taught in the schools.[4] (And this survey was conducted before the current concern with AIDS.) Similarly, attacks on library collections may generate a fair amount of noise, but the great majority of your fellow citizens are much more temperate and reasonable in their views.

2. Get organized.

In some ways a school resource center is a bit like a department store. A department store has a wide variety of goods to offer its customers, just as a resource center has a wide variety of books and other materials to offer its readers. Most of the goods in the store will satisfy the customers; some, however, will be found unsatisfactory. Can you imagine a department store without a complaint department or a complaint procedure? — a store in which each complaint comes as a shock and is treated on an *ad hoc* basis? This is exactly what is happening in many schools. There is no collection policy and no way to deal with challenges to the collection. Jenkinson found on his scorecard of Manitoba censorship challenges, that in schools which had collection policies, about one-third more materials were retained after challenges than remained in resource centers in those schools without policies. A good, written collection policy is your first line of defense, and any resource center without such a document is running at grave risk.

How do you acquire a collection policy? Some teacher-librarians simply copy another school's policy and declare it their own. This is a weak strategy. Remember that the object of the exercise is to broaden your base of support. This is best achieved through a cooperative process of shared ownership. By omitting this process you have done little to strengthen your position. The critic will move easily from attacking you and the collection, to attacking the collection policy, which will be portrayed as simply an expression of your personal philosophy. It is much better to take the longer and somewhat more difficult route of working together with your colleagues and administrators to develop an original, in-house document. With this in place, the critic will no longer be attacking you alone, but will be challenging the collection policy drawn up and supported by the teachers and the principal. You should, however, go further in strengthening your position. A process that involves not only the teachers and administrators, but also includes the students, and parents and community representatives will do far more to broaden the base of your support. This will be a time consuming process, but the result will provide a strong measure of security. It is an opportunity for you to explain how the library resource center functions in the education process and the importance of intellectual freedom. It is a time to marshal supporters for the school library. A collection development committee should include influential community representatives: for example, writers or media people will bring their special interests to bear; a public health nurse will be able to speak to the need for health and human development materials in the collection; parents will share their knowledge of the community and its concerns; students will provide a voice from that quarter; and a lawyer will give advice on drawing up the document and procedures. The committee must necessarily be limited to a reasonable-sized working group, but broad representation is recommended, and any steps to involve others—the PTA, social agencies,

special interest groups—by inviting presentations or requesting input on portions of the policy will pay dividends. As in any democratic process, there will be compromises made, and the final document may not conform entirely to your own viewpoint. In the end, however, you will have acquired a clear understanding of the school and community's view of your resource center and its function; you will have had an opportunity to communicate your professional concerns and beliefs to your colleagues and the community; you will have built a network of supporters; and you will have cooperatively constructed a policy and process to provide defense in the event of a challenge to the collection. A detailed description of one version of this cooperative approach may be found in Van Orden's *The Collection Program in High Schools*,[13] or in her *The Collection Program in Elementary and Middle Schools*.[12]

It is important that the completed document be presented to the school board (or other governing body) for approval and support. A statement such as, "Approved by the Board of School Trustees of School District X" affixed to the cover of the collection policy clearly indicates the corporate backing for the document, and thus adds to its power.

Although duplication of another school's selection policy is not recommended, it is, nevertheless, rewarding to examine examples of existing policies. These have generally been drawn up with care, after considerable thought and consideration, and much can be learned from a close study of their contents and wording. Examples of resource center collection policies (or applicable portions of other policies, such as a gift or weeding procedures) are to be found in a number of sources:

- Taylor's *School Library and Media Center Acquisition Policies and Procedures*[11] contains a number of full and partial selection policies, as well as the full text of the important American Library Association policies which bear on intellectual freedom and which you may wish to include in your collection policy document. The Freedom to Read Statement and the Library Bill of Rights are examples of such statements.

- Futas' thick volume, *Library Acquisition Policies and Procedures*[3] contains a large number of examples of academic and public library policies. Portions of these policies, such as those dealing with principles of selection, and selection criteria, will be of use to teacher-librarians. Appendices include a number of the important ALA policy statements.

- Davis' *Dealing with Censorship*[2] contains contributed articles on all aspects of censorship, including schools; of particular interest is the Donelson article, written from the viewpoint of an English teacher, on how to handle censorship. Davis also includes the full text of an excellent model policy developed by the Iowa Department of Public Instruction.

- Jones' *Defusing Censorship: The Librarian's Guide to Handling Censorship Conflicts*[7] has a section on school resource centers, with a particularly interesting article on coping with conflict, including internal censorship. The appendix has a list of places to turn for help, and guidelines for writing a materials selection policy.

- Van Orden's *The Collection Program in Elementary and Middle Schools*[12] is a general text with chapters on intellectual freedom and policies and procedures. The chapters on developing policy statements is very useful. It describes the steps to be taken, presents a model selection policy (the well-regarded Iowa policy), and identifies other policies and guides. Highly recommended. (This material is also available in Van Orden's *The Collection Program in High Schools*.[13])

- The *Intellectual Freedom Manual*[5] published by the ALA is an essential purchase. It gives all the relevant ALA statements, and has a section on school libraries and intellectual freedom. Most helpful is the chapter entitled "Before the Censor Comes: Essential Preparations." The chapter on public relations and the library contains suggestions not found elsewhere. This is also the source of a new, much improved, complaint form.

- Stanek's *Censorship: A Guide for Teachers, Librarians and Others Concerned with Intellectual Freedom*[10] is a low cost pamphlet available from Dell publishers. It is an excellent compilation of useful information, including ALA position statements, as well as those of the Association of American Publishers, the National Council of Teachers of English and the American Civil Liberties Union. It also contains two different examples of reconsideration forms.

- *Censorship: Stopping the Book Banners*[1] is one of the few Canadian resources available. It is a low cost booklet published by the Book and Periodical Development Council. It contains a wealth of information, including the Freedom of Expression and the Freedom to Read statements developed by the Book and Periodical Council, and endorsed by Canadian publishers', writers' and librarians' associations, and the Canadian Library Association Statement on intellectual freedom. There is also a list of banned books, newspaper columns regarding the banning of *The Diviners* in Ontario, an open letter to teachers from Margaret Laurence, a strategy for countering censors, a sample reconsideration form, and a list of resources and readings.

- One of the best examples of a collection policy, and one of the most readily available, is the policy statement developed by the Vancouver (British Columbia) School Board and published in full in *Emergency Librarian* (*EL*, 12:1 [September-October, 1984], pages 23-26).

By cooperatively developing a collection policy you will have firmly welded together the upper two blocks of the pyramid, thus greatly increasing your strength. To further broaden your base of support it is necessary to establish an ongoing program of public relations. This program will have several objectives:

- To demonstrate the importance of the school resource center and how it operates

- to make firm friends and allies for the resource center

- to form links with individuals and organizations that would provide support in times of trouble

- to do all of the above well *before a* censorship controversy arises.

What form should a public relations program take? To whom should it be directed? Within the school you will want to conduct inservice programs and informal discussions with the staff and administrators. Because of turnover in staffing it is a good practice to review the selection policy with the teaching staff annually. This is best done as a joint presentation with the principal.

More broadly, parents can be reached through open house days, through parent volunteers, or by means of a library newsletter. Inclusion of parents on the collection policy committee and the reconsideration committee is an excellent way to build links.

Public relations implies something much more inclusive than a concern with censorship and intellectual freedom. Indeed, the main objective of a public relations program is to demonstrate the importance and involvement of the teacher-librarian and resource center in the educational process. By inviting poets, writers, illustrators, publishers and other outside parties to give talks and presentations in the resource center, you involve them with the program. They learn about the things that you are doing and become part of the resource center. You can build upon this by keeping in contact with their organizations and advising them of your activities and problems. Such organizations as local, state or provincial writers' federations are especially aware of censorship, and often have their own well-developed mechanisms and contacts to cope with this problem. They can be strong allies.

Teacher-librarians are too modest about their accomplishments. The local news media should be invited to report on writers' visits, book clubs and other activities. Learn how to write press releases. In this way, you make yourself known to the media. Many teacher-librarians, after working hard to develop a collection policy, secret it away in a desk drawer, only to be produced should the occasion demand. You should publicize the policy. It is, after all, something upon which you and your committee and the board have worked hard. It is something to be proud of, and people should be informed of your achievements.

Finally, it is a good idea to discover whether your local, state, or provincial library organizations have committees concerned with the defense of intellectual freedom. If they do not it is time that they took action on this. An initial step might be to establish a registry of censorship challenges. Jenkinson's survey is particularly valuable for the depth of information which it provides. He was able to gather the following details about each of the items challenged: author; title; urban or rural site of the library concerned; nature of complaint; category of complainant; whether or not the library had a collection policy, and whether it was a written policy; the degree to which the policy was followed—ranging from (^{1}) policy followed not at all to (^{5}) policy followed fully; and the outcome of the challenge. The uniform use (with permission) of the Jenkinson instrument for the systematic collection of such data would allow comparisons to be made on an annual basis, and between provinces or states. Publication of the results would also inform the public of the problem.

With a successful public relations program in place, the third block of the pyramid will be securely bonded to the other two, forming a strong structure which will act to protect you and to advance the cause of intellectual freedom in the schools. Teacher-librarians who do not have a plan of defense against censors are irresponsible, and possibly suicidal. Make your plans now.

NOTES

1. Book and Periodical Development Council, n.d. *Censorship: Stopping the Book Banners.*

2. Davis, James E. ed. *Dealing with Censorship.* National Council of Teachers of English, 1979.

3. Futas, Elizabeth. *Library Acquisition Policies and Procedures.* Oryx Press, 1984.

4. "Gallup Poll Reveals Attitudes toward Sexuality." *Tellus,* volume 5, number 3 (Autumn, 1984), page 25.

5. *Intellectual Freedom Manual.* 2d ed. American Library Association, 1983.

6. Jenkinson, David. "Censorship Iceberg: Results of a Survey of Challenges in Public and School Libraries." *Canadian Library Journal,* volume 43, number 1 (February, 1986), pages 7-21.

7. Jones, Frances M. *Defusing Censorship: The Librarian's Guide to Handling Censorship Conflicts.* Oryx Press, 1983.

8. "Newsletter on Intellectual Freedom." American Library Association. Bimonthly. Specifically: volume 35, number 2 (March, 1986).

9. Schrader, Alvin M. and Keith Walker. "Censorship Iceberg: Results of an Alberta Public Library Survey." *Canadian Library Journal,* volume 43, number 2 (April, 1986), pages 91-95.

10. Stanek, Lou Willet. *Censorship: A Guide for Teachers, Librarians, and Others Concerned with Intellectual Freedom.* Dell, n.d.

11. Taylor, Mary M., ed. *School Library and Media Center Acquisition Policies and Procedures.* Oryx Press, 1981.

12. Van Orden, Phyllis J. *The Collection Program in Elementary and Middle Schools.* Libraries Unlimited, 1982, pages 104-20.

13. Van Orden, Phyllis J. *The Collection Program in High Schools.* Libraries Unlimited, 1985, pages 90-108.

Analyzing and Assessing Programs and Services
Science/Resource Center Principles:
For Every Action There Is a Reaction

Linda Dunlop and Julie Andreacchi

INTRODUCTION

Close examination of class use of the resource center can be a useful tool to determine the extent to which library and classroom activities form a planned, integrated teaching program. Specific focus is given here to the teaching of science.

PROBLEM IDENTIFICATION

A specific problem was identified in our resource center — the seeming lack of involvement of members of the science department in resource-based teaching and learning — the science program and the library program were less well-integrated than others.

The problem affected the library environment in three important areas: teaching staff, students, and the collection. For example:

- Provincial guidelines issued by the Ministry of Education emphasize close cooperation between classroom teachers and teacher-librarians. This means that classroom teachers in all departments (or, at least, the 80% factor) work closely with the resource center; this increases teacher-librarian credibility and helps to alleviate the unnecessary frustration which results when the competencies of the teacher-librarian are not fully realized.

- Students have a tendency to have a one-dimensional view of the resource center: it's for certain subjects only, and most of those subjects are related to the arts and humanities rather than the sciences. Students learn best by example; presumably, if science teachers became involved, students, too, would have their horizons broadened—there's more to science than labs and classroom textbooks.

- The science collection is sizable, but its potential is not being realized. Also, with newer approaches to science, it would be useful to augment and supplement the collection. To do so would require additional funds. Increased cooperation would assist in the acquisition and wise expenditure of these funds.

EXTERNAL CONSIDERATIONS

The extent of involvement of the science department, and the extent to which the library program is integrated with the science program, depend on factors beyond the scope of the personnel and materials available in either the resource center or the science department. It is sometimes too easy to blame ourselves or others for a seeming lack of accomplishment, or to feel that there are no roadblocks if we set our minds to accomplishing something.

The following are a few of the external considerations that impact on this problem:

Time is a constant consideration and is nothing to be ashamed of. Everyone, including the teacher-librarian and science teacher, has only a certain amount of time available. Priorities must be carefully established.

Workload is related to time. For science teachers, there are plenty of lab reports to mark. Is a partnership with the resource center thought of in terms of an increase in workload; one more thing to mark? Can time spent generating new ideas be spent on other things instead?

Money in limited amounts is always a consideration, especially in times of budget restraint. There is a tendency to allocate funds to departments which make greatest use. Which should come first? Expenditure of funds (and energy) to entice prospective customers, or a trusted and steady clientele before the "extras" are added?

Cutbacks in staffing may cause the teacher-librarian to assume the role of a technician where survival and not cooperative program planning and teaching is the number one priority. It is imperative that the principal of the school has a complete understanding of cooperative program planning and teaching so that a message of support through staffing allocations is conveyed to the various departments in the school.

GOALS OF THE STUDY

In order to determine the validity of the perceived problem, an evaluative study was designed to determine the extent to which the school library program is integrated with the science program. Evaluation of services in terms of the expressed needs of the present users would not be as helpful as examining non-users; in other words, a look at the English departments where good and extensive integration takes place, would not prove as helpful as a look at a program in which participation is at a different level. The following goals were set for our evaluative study:

- To determine the extent to which the school library program is integrated with the science program.

- To encourage the teachers of science and, hence, the students in science courses to become enthusiastic participants in resource-based teaching and learning.

OBJECTIVES OF THE STUDY

- The teacher-librarian will know the level of involvement of science teachers with the resource center for the past few years.

- The teacher-librarian will become aware of the expectations of members of the science department for library-based learning now and in the future.

- The teacher-librarian will become aware of the level of familiarity of science teachers with the teaching services and collection available in the resource center.

- The teacher-librarian will embark on a course of action based on this information in order to increase the integration of the school resource center with the science program.

EVALUATIVE INSTRUMENTS AND ANALYSIS OF RESULTS

To accomplish the goals and objectives of this evaluative study, two instruments were employed—a user study and the interview.

A User Study. To measure quantitatively levels of involvement, library reports from the past six years were gathered and analyzed. The statistics helped determine the extent to which the resource center and science program are integrated. For example:

Year I (six years ago)—science department visits to the resource center represented 4% of the total number of classroom visits in that year

Year II—science department visits represented 6.4% of the total

Year III—science department visits represented 4% of the total

Year IV—science department visits represented 7.6% of the total

Year V—science department visits represented 2% of the total

Year VI (most recent)—science department visits represented 2.5% of the total

Although some fluctuation exists, it is apparent that the problem as originally identified does indeed exist. The fluctuation occurs at the lower end of the scale. There is less involvement on the part of the members of the science department in library-based programs than on the part of the members of other departments; the science program is less well integrated with the resource center than are others.

The Interview. To determine qualitatively the current level of involvement, as well as to give the teacher-librarian some idea of the present situation and direction for the future, personal interviews were set up. Opinions rather than evidence were sought through this process.

The personal interviews were pleasant and productive. Cooperation from the members of the science department was 100%. They were more than generous with their time and eager to share their perceptions. Questions such as "How frequently do you use the resource center? What are the factors that influence your use of the center? How aware are you of the current teaching program and the collection available?" were posed. The information gleaned can be summarized as follows.

Communication. As in most issues, communication figured prominently in the conversations. Both departments (science and resource center) were operating on independent tracks, often oblivious to the goals and objectives of the other. From the point of view of the science teachers interviewed, cooperative program planning and teaching was not fully understood and thus not considered a priority.

Familiarity with the collection and teaching services available in the resource center varied, but tended toward the limited and were dependent on the initiative of the teacher-librarian rather than of the science teacher. Occasional forays into the resource center to glance at recommended or required materials was the most frequently cited use on the initiative of the science teacher.

Teacher and *Learning Styles.* An interesting revelation was the number of times that the variance in teaching styles on the part of the science teachers and the teacher-librarian was cited. In some instances, the teacher-librarian was viewed as being in the position of having the luxury of time to be creative and, therefore, at odds with the more traditional expectations of the science teacher; and, in other instances, the teacher-librarian was viewed as being too restrictive and possessing a style not conducive to the learning that the teacher desired for students. This variance was viewed quite negatively on the part of some of those interviewed. In effect, because of familiarity with the teaching services offered, some chose to decline those services.

Materials. The heavy emphasis on "the textbook" in science classes has a limiting effect on those wishing to avail themselves of the resource center's collection and services. Furthermore, the members of the science department indicated their satisfaction with their own well-stocked department. Class sets of supplementary textbooks, film loops, and reference books are all readily available to them. If there is a need for additional material from the resource center (and this is its primary function according to those interviewed), it appears to be for current information both in content and in form. There was also an expressed need for sufficient quantities of materials, sometimes a difficulty where a few, expensive scientific books and encyclopedias constitute the backbone of the collection.

Time. "I'm always pushing to get the course covered," was the common complaint. The sentiment was phrased by one teacher in this way, "I shy away from extra things, especially things that are bookish."

The pervading opinion was that science has a unique focus with time spent in a lab setting where students are hypothesizing, collecting data, interpreting data, and writing conclusions; the emphasis should be on these skills. If research skills are taught by the teacher-librarian in other classes, why should science classes have the information repeated? The concern was that somehow the teacher-librarian's agenda would impose on that of the science teacher.

Fairly positive feedback was received from those interviewed, however. The science teachers were far less critical of the resource center than we of them and of ourselves. This is probably owing to our heightened awareness of the possibilities that exist and our zest for conversion. The following two phrases best typify the prevailing attitude of the science department towards the resource center—"The machine works, why fix it?" and, conversely, on occasion, "The machine isn't working, but I can't figure out how to make it work."

RECOMMENDATIONS AND/OR SOLUTIONS

Findings confirm that cooperative program planning and teaching with science teachers is weak. From the point of view of the teacher-librarian, what can be done to encourage the teachers of science (and their students) to become enthusiastic participants in resource-based teaching and learning through the resource center?

The recommendations fall into four categories based on this analysis:

Communication. The teacher-librarian must take the initiative in defining the role of the school librarian as a professional teaching partner, through cooperative program planning and teaching. More in-service and public relations work is an absolute necessity.

Curriculum. The teacher-librarian must have a clear understanding of his/her own program priorities and curriculum entry points before it is possible to communicate this to others. In our investigation such an understanding did not always present itself.

The teacher-librarian must also be committed to understanding the curriculum in departments like science where there is the hope of increased involvement. The teacher-librarian must become aware of the present curriculum and of any changes anticipated.

Collection. The teacher-librarian must constantly assess the collection for appropriateness and relevance. In terms of the science collection, materials must be as up-to-date as as possible. Cooperation with the members of the science department over purchases to be made or topics on which to stay current is recommended. Such cooperation and discussion should focus on intended use.

Creativity. The teacher-librarian must not be locked into certain ways of doing things. It is essential to stay abreast of current teaching strategies and to remain open to change. Every teacher-librarian should be a risk-taker.

There is a commitment on the part of the teacher-librarian to cooperative program planning and teaching. There is no doubt that this priority is working in some departments and with some teachers. As our study showed, however, it is not working as effectively in the science department. It must be reemphasized and clarified; it is important to take stock occasionally and to recommit ourselves to the task.

NEW ACTION

As a result of the foregoing, the following suggestions for new action are being examined. Many of the suggestions have been tried before. Some of the suggestions may meet with frustration when attempts are made to initiate them. However, the process may be just as important as the finished product. There is much to learn.

Teacher-librarians should strive to meet personal and professional goals.

Communication

- attend science department meetings to stay current, to assess needs, and to contribute support

- submit articles on cooperative program planning to professional science education journals: articles should explain the concept and the need for involvement on the part of science teachers

- offer in-sessions on cooperative program planning and teaching

- invite the school library consultant and the science consultant to offer a joint in-session for subject teachers and teacher-librarians

- coordinate a joint session with teachers in a department where there is a heavy involvement in resource-based teaching and learning, and with members of the science department where more involvement is desirable

- develop an interdisciplinary unit as a result of the joint sessions

- target one receptive member of the department and develop a unit; other members learn by example, rather than by pressure

- invite the principal or department head to view resource-based learning in action in order to tout the merits of the program to others

- convey the advantages of resource-based learning at every opportunity (develop a list of ideas)

Curriculum

- get a copy of each course of study offered in the science department and study it carefully; highlight areas where the content will lend itself to resource-based learning

- develop and establish a joint skills continuum

- integrate each grade level into the skills continuum so that the variety of skills are taught with a minimum of duplication

- sit in on science classes to better understand the curriculum, methodology, and teaching styles of science teachers

- evaluate entire assignments (or parts thereof) that have been cooperatively planned to date to establish better credibility as a teacher-librarian

Collection

- have a representative(s) from the science department and/or administration assist in the selection of materials so that the collection is current and meets the needs of the curriculum

- evaluate the use of the science collection; weed and augment according to user statistics, not whim

- start or maintain a vertical information file—an inexpensive source of up-to-date information

- subscribe to appropriate scientific periodicals in lieu of purchasing expensive texts that become dated quickly

- purchase software and audio-visual materials in order to maintain a multi-sensory approach that caters to different learning styles

Creativity

- display science work done by students; ask science teachers and students to assist in a display of scientific materials

- plan for half the class in the laboratory with the science teacher and half the class with the teacher-librarian to extend the unit in the resource center

- implement a unit which allows science teachers and students to broaden their scope; e.g., extend a topic to cover some controversial material involving value judgments that affect "real" life

CONCLUSION

These suggestions are by no means exhaustive but they, along with the other information contained in this study, can be used as an impetus for discussion and eventual involvement of science teachers and science students in resource-based teaching and learning.

And then, there are the members of the mathematics department.

Building Consensus and Power in the Library Community
The Marketing of School Library Services by a Provincial Library Association

Robin Inskip

Alberta school libraries have been the focus of a province-wide public awareness campaign since publication of the Alberta Education *Position Paper on Alberta School Libraries* in March, 1983. The Library Association of Alberta (LAA) built the campaign as a lead in and follow-up to the LAA's first brief to the Education Caucus Committee of the provincial legislature on June 22, 1983. Based on the positive response from government and the community, LAA's second annual brief on February 15, 1983 concentrated on educational policy changes needed for school libraries.

The purpose of this article is to outline briefly the marketing of school libraries by a provincial library association. The article will explore how basic marketing and organizational behaviour theories can be applied to a library marketing problem.

MARKETING FOR NONPROFIT ORGANIZATIONS

The LAA marketing process can be examined in terms of services marketing, legislative marketing (lobbying) and social marketing.

The key text, Philip Kolter's *Marketing for Nonprofit Organizations* defines a service as:

> ...any activity or benefit that one party can offer to another that is essentially intangible and does not result in the ownership of anything. Its production may or may not be tied to a physical product.[3:477]

The important consideration of services marketing in this context is intangibility. The thrust of the LAA brief and the public awareness campaign was the crucial contribution of qualified teacher-librarians to school instructional programs and the education of students. A recent research paper by

Dr. Philomena Hauck, professor of education at the University of Calgary, states that university courses for teachers and school administrators barely mention libraries and methodology textbooks are silent on the subject.[2] Since most decision-makers—legislators, Department of Education staff, school administrators and teachers—have never experienced the benefits of professionally directed school library service, the concept needed to be marketed as an innovation.

Lobbying or legislative marketing calls for a comprehensive examination of:

- organizational buying behaviour (how policy is developed: the roles of the Minister, Deputy Minister, library policy researchers in provincial departments, caucus committees and individual legislators);

- consumer buying behavior (how decision-makers think, feel, act);

- marketing strategy development (how to select target decision-makers and influence the individual or organizational behaviour)[3:451]

The term "social marketing," according to Kolter, was first introduced in 1971 to describe the use of marketing principles and techniques to advance a social cause, idea, or behaviour. Social marketing is:

> ...the design, implementation, and control of programs seeking to increase the acceptability of a social idea or cause in a target group(s). It utilizes concepts of market segmentation, consumer research, concept development, communication, facilitation, incentives and exchange theory to maximize target group response.[3:490]

The central theory of marketing is exchange. Each party can offer something that the other perceives to be of value;

each is capable of communication with the other; each can deliver its offered value, and the trade is assumed to leave both parties better off.[3:37]

The provincial government decision-makers can perceive the exchange benefits of the provincial library association as a source of ideas and community concerns, feedback mechanism for their policy proposals, and a communications channel to the association members, and other organizations, individuals and the media for marketing the government's ideas. Other decision-makers in high priority associations and boards, such as the Learning Resources Council (LRC) of the Alberta Teachers' Association (ATA), the Alberta Library Trustees Association (ALTA) and the Alberta Library Board (advisory to the Minister of Culture), can perceive the same set of exchange relationships.

Marketing process and procedure involves segmenting target markets, identifying the needs of target markets, offering the product (idea) in terms of target markets' needs and values, planning strategies and tactics organized to the concepts of product (idea), price (can be psychological or social price of not accepting the product), place or distribution (influence channel analysis for decision-makers) and promotion (types of formal and informal communication required to influence behaviour) and evaluating the results of the marketing program.[3:510-514]

SITUATION ANALYSIS FOR ALBERTA SCHOOL LIBRARIES IN 1983

David King, Minister of Education, ordered a Departmental Task Force on School Libraries in 1982. The Task Force issued the March 1983 *Position Paper on Alberta School Libraries*. The Position Paper stated that students are not receiving the school library services they need or deserve and called for provincial leadership in policy development, school libraries with professional teacher-librarians in charge and recognition that the primary role of the school library should be to provide services, facilities and materials that are fully integrated into the instructional program.

As mentioned previously, the idea of the benefits of provincial policy for professionally directed school library services and cooperative curriculum planning by teachers and teacher-librarians was an innovation to almost all target markets.

It is worth noting that the *Position Paper* originally had a limited distribution to what Alberta Education (the provincial department of education) considered the major stakeholder groups: Alberta Teachers' Association, Alberta School Trustees Association, etc. The LAA and other organizations interested in library development or educational policy (such as the Alberta Library Trustees Association or Alberta Association for Continuing Education) did not receive copies of the *Position Paper* in the original mailing. As well, Alberta Education did not conduct any public relations/communications efforts to raise public awareness. Alberta Education took a low key approach to community response to the *Position Paper*.

The Learning Resources Council is a specialist division for teacher-librarians and others in the Alberta Teachers' Association. The ATA is on record as supporting library services and teacher-librarians and sponsored a Symposium on School

Libraries in May, 1983. At the time of mobilizing public support after the *Position Paper*, however, the ATA was occupied in establishing its positions on proposed provincial compulsory departmental exams and the firing of Jim Keegstra in Eckville. The concerns of school libraries were in competition with other urgent organizational priorities. As well, in 1983 the LAA had the opportunity, unique in the library community, to present a brief and accompanying background book to the Education Caucus Committee.

An indication of the difficult situation for Alberta school libraries is apparent in the following list, based on Alberta Education estimates:

- in the last three years, 100 schools cut their teacher-librarian positions

- 55 percent of the school libraries have clerks rather than professional teacher-librarians in charge

- only three school districts have a full-time library coordinator with library science and instructional media qualifications

- 92 percent of the teachers in charge of libraries have less than the minimum qualifications recommended by the Learning Resources Council of the Alberta Teachers' Association.

Four marketing opportunities occurred. The Minister of Education David King spoke to the annual LAA Conference in April, 1983. Mr. King stated that learning quickly outdated facts was inappropriate. Learning how to learn was important in an information society. From that perspective, Mr. King said that school libraries are essential to the process of education.

On May 12, 1983 a private member's bill on school library standards (Motion 211 in Alberta *Hansard*) demonstrated strong political support for improving school libraries. It is interesting to note that the majority of speakers to this motion were members of the Caucus Committee on Health and Social Services which has the responsibility for public library policy review.

A press release was issued for both of these occasions to be positive for the politicians and to restate the LAA position.

Alberta media gave considerable press coverage of the firing of Jim Keegstra, a former social studies teacher in Eckville. Mr. Keegstra was dismissed because the school board decided that Mr. Keegstra was not following the Alberta curriculum and that he was teaching the events of World War II in a biased manner. Mr. Keegstra taught that the Holocaust did not occur.

The LAA noted that Mr. Keegstra frequently was photographed surrounded by the books he used as authorities for his teaching. LAA issued a press release stating that one way that the Alberta government could increase tolerance and understanding was to improve school libraries. Students would have access to mainstream historical analysis and learn independent research skills to make up their own minds.

A 1983 *Discussion Paper* by Alberta Advanced Education states that a change in education policy and an increased emphasis on libraries, including network services between libraries, are needed for:

...a process of lifelong human learning with the individual being assisted in his learning by freely accessing learning materials and participating in both organized and non-formal learning activities.[1:12]

The author of the Discussion Paper, Dr. Des Berghofer, is the Assistant Deputy Minister responsible for policy on further education and university and college libraries. The Discussion Paper's quote was worked into the brief. Dr. Berghofer was invited to a LAA executive meeting.

PROBLEM DEFINITION

The key problem was to communicate the benefits of intangible school library services in terms that the target markets could understand and accept. The target would also need to understand the price of not accepting the benefits.

GOAL SETTING

Four goals were identified:

1. To persuade the provincial government to publish policy and guidelines for school libraries.

2. To present the 'product concept' of the idea that schools are failing to educate their students in information retrieval and research skills. This failure in school library programs results in students being denied the skills they need for lifelong learning and creates problems for university, college and public libraries. The bottom line is that many students cannot get information for their assignments. In an Age of Information, "Johnny can't retrieve information."

3. To communicate the product concept model to selected target markets through formal and informal means.

4. To request and evaluate feedback.

TARGET MARKET SEGMENTATION AND CONSUMER ANALYSIS

Targets are segmented by type, and then by analysis of needs of each segment.

1. **Provincial Politicians and Civil Servants**
    The three Ministries and caucus committees needed to be informed of the benefits of change. The targets were:

    - Minister, Deputy Minister, Assistant Deputy Minister or Director, and policy researchers of Alberta Education, Alberta Advanced Education and Alberta Culture.

    - Caucus Committee on Education (schools, universities and college policies)

    - Caucus Committee on Health and Social Services (public library policy)

    - Opposition MLAs.

    The key benefits to this group were the 'good feelings' of leadership and contribution to the improvement of educating children. Recognition of their positive actions and statements was required, and executed through communications reinforcement to library and educational organizations, constituents, and the media.

2. **Educational Associations and Organizations**
    Communications about the benefits of the innovative idea of the school library as an integrative curriculum agency were required. The impact of the failure of schools to provide library programs and the importance of school libraries to the Minister of Education and influential MLAs were vital psychological and social price considerations for this group. These targets could be motivated to be able to react in public forums and the media to initiatives by LAA and other organizations. The targets were:

    - Alberta Teachers' Association

    - Alberta School Trustees' Association

    - Alberta Council of School Administrators

    - Alberta Federation of Home and School Associations

    - Alberta Association of Continuing Education.

3. **Library Associations**
    Library associations and organizations' support of the product idea at the provincial and local level was imperative. The product concept was presented as a mutual exchange of values and benefits to all sectors of the Alberta library community. The targets were:

    - Library Association of Alberta

    - Learning Resources Council of the ATA

    - Alberta Library Trustees Association

    - Alberta Library Board

    - Alberta Universities Librarians

    - Alberta Public Libraries Directors Council

    - Association of Community College Librarians

    - Canadian Association of Special Libraries and Information Services Chapters in Edmonton and Calgary

    - Alberta Government Librarians' Council

    - Edmonton Library Association

    - Foothills Library Association (Calgary area)

    - Canadian Library Association

4. **Municipal and Rural Government Associations**
   This target group has a strong interest in schools. They are responsible for local funding and policy support for public libraries. Since the product concept was lifelong learning and the interrelationship of the roles of school and public libraries, this group was important. The targets would be attracted to the 'good feelings' of supporting the improvement of their communities by the development of school and public libraries as educational and cultural agencies. The targets were:

   - Alberta Chambers of Commerce
   - Alberta Urban Municipalities Association
   - Alberta Association of Rural Municipalities
   - Association of Municipal Districts and Counties

5. **Post Secondary Education Decision Makers**
   Presidents and their executives determine funding and policy for universities and college libraries. This group's stake is the student's ability to conduct scholarly independent research and capability of accessing research material. Deans of faculties of education may wish to graduate a better product. The targets were:

   - Presidents of colleges and universities
   - Deans of faculties of education

6. **Media**
   The focus of the campaign for media was to get them to publish not only our recommendations but also the problem set or product concept that students are not learning independent research skills. The LAA's 'hottest' news release on how school libraries could combat racism was timed to be close to the brief presentation. The targets were:

   - Dailies in Alberta cities
   - Weeklies located in the constituencies of the three Ministers and MLAs on both Education and Health Social Services Caucus Committees
   - *Letter of the LAA, LRC Newsletter, Quill and Quire, Feliciter*
   - Radio (especially CBC)
   - *New Trail*, the University of Alberta Alumni magazine

INFLUENCE CHANNEL ANALYSES

Social marketers need the cooperation of a number of influence channels to carry out their programs. The attitude of the majority of influence channels has been examined in the preceding section on target market segmentation.

However, one of the frequently used keys is to take social marketing campaigns down to the grassroots level. The LAA used two avenues to facilitate this mechanism.

Public librarians in each city with a daily newspaper were asked to take the LAA background book to the 1983 brief to the editor two weeks in advance of the presentation. The public librarian followed up with the brief on the day of presentation. The LAA hoped to build a local media contact network through these steps. As well, the LAA requested that the public librarians contact teacher-librarians in the community and be their spokesperson. In this fashion we hoped to provide a local spokesperson without a conflict of interest on school library issues.

The author gave a paper to the LRC Conference on May 28, 1983. The paper presented the marketing of school libraries as an issue for the October, 1983 school boards and municipal elections. The LRC speech followed the same model as this article. It suggested the establishment of local Citizens' Committees for Libraries and Lifelong Learning composed of teacher-librarians, teachers, sympathetic school trustees and parents, public librarians, and public library trustees. The speech also recommended that teacher-librarians and school trustees also speak out in favor of public libraries. Again, the advantages of mutual exchange and support were stressed. The Citizens' Committees' target audiences would include not only local candidates for school board and municipal elections and the media but also target market segment, *1. Provincial Politicians and Civil Servants*. The speech recommended writing letters and asking for an appointment with the MLA at his constituency office. (In fact, local citizen committees did form in seven cities.)

MARKETING STRATEGY AND TACTICS

A short review of the four "p's" of the marketing program may be in order.

Product
The idea that schools are failing to educate their students in independent research and study skills.

Price
Decision makers can hardly choose not to facilitate improvements in students' education in the face of the information explosion and rapidly shifting education, technology, and occupation environments.

Place
The distribution was by

- the formal presentation of the brief and background book to the MLAs on the Caucus Committee on Education
- sending brief and background book to all identified target markets
- press releases before and after brief. Press releases on Mr. King's speech, the private member's bill and Mr. Keegstra all led into the press release on the brief. They were sent to target segments (1) provincial politicians and civil servants, (2) educational associations and organizations, (3) library associations as well as the media, (4) municipal and rural governments, and (5) post secondary education decision-makers

- follow up suggestion of articles in *New Trail* (Winter, 1983) and *Quill and Quire* (scheduled for the February, 1984 Special Issue on Education)

Promotion

The major 1983 communications vehicles were the brief, background book and press releases. The 82 page background book had several purposes: to present the theme of libraries and lifelong learning in general, and for each type of library (school, university and college, public and special); to provide summaries of important policies and statistical breakdowns for each type of library; to present current newspaper articles on library issues; to note MLAs' legislative speeches on libraries by copying Alberta *Hansard*.

The brief and background book were placed in folders. Personal labels were attached to the file folder package: i.e. LAA Background Materials for the 1983 Brief to the Education Caucus Committee. Prepared for William Thorsell, Assistant Editor, *Edmonton Journal*.

Personal letters, together with press releases, were mailed to each individual. The editors of all media were identified, as well as city editors for daily newspapers. Civil servants' titles were confirmed. Presidents or executive directors of associations were added to the LAA mailing list.

PROGRAM REVIEW AND EVALUATION

Social marketing programs evaluation is the assessment of the behaviour of target organizations and individuals.

The first indication of change was the Alberta School Trustees Association.

In television, radio, and newspaper interviews at the trustees' fall 1983 convention the ASTA President reacted to the Department of Education's announcement that 1984 provincial school grants would be frozen at 1983 levels, by stating that school boards would be pressed hard to preserve school programs, including "saving our libraries."

The Department of Education received 90 responses to the March 1983 *Position Paper*. There were 20 responses from associations and institutions and 70 from individuals.

Dr. Frank Crowther, Director, Edmonton Region, Alberta Education, and chair of the task force, said that the responses were very positive.[4] Based on these responses the Department decided that the Position Paper should have the status of a Green Paper. (A Green Paper has more government status than a position paper; its purpose is to explore officially community response to a new idea or initiative.) Alberta Education re-established the Departmental Task Force that researched and wrote the Position Paper and plans to issue a White Paper on school libraries in May, 1984.

The White Paper will have three components:

(1) statements of appropriate policy and guidelines for provincial, school district, and school levels.

(2) standards for school libraries.

(3) a service document which would stimulate ideas on how to establish high quality school library services by providing models drawn from effective school library examples in the province.

The February 15, 1984 LAA brief followed the same marketing process as the presentation of the 1983 brief to the Education Caucus Committee. It applauded the leadership of Alberta Education and recommended wide distribution of the upcoming Paper, and publication of provincial policy and standards for school libraries after community response.

There are two limitations on this good news from Alberta Education. The first reality is that the Alberta Government's philosophical position leans towards local autonomy rather than provincial imposition. To make the proposed provincial policies work, a major change process must also be sponsored. To alter the planning process for instructional programs, the individual teacher, teacher-librarian or school administrator must change perceptions of, and values attached to, school library services.

The 1983 LAA brief recommended that Alberta Education plan and fund major multiyear educational programs for teachers, teacher-librarians and school and district administrators. As well the new brief recommended financial incentives through special provincial funding to encourage schools to adopt and integrate excellent school library services in their support of the Alberta school curriculum.

The LAA's 1983-84 social marketing program for school libraries should lead to improvements in school library services in the province. In addition the marketing program provides an opportunity to meet some of the important constitutional objectives of the Library Association of Alberta.

SOURCES

1. *Development of Education Policy in the Context of Lifelong Learning*. Discussion Paper by Desmond E. Berghofer. Edmonton: Alberta Advanced Education, March 2, 1983.

2. Hauck, Philomena, Joe Forsyth and Bruce Peel. "History of Libraries in Alberta" in *Libraries 2000, A Symposium Sponsored by the Alberta Library Board*. Edmonton: Alberta Library Board, in press. (Alberta Culture may be the government agency publisher.)

3. Kolter, Philip, *Marketing for Nonprofit Organizations*, 2nd edition. Englewood Cliffs, New Jersey: Prentice-Hall, 1982.

4. Telephone interview with Dr. Frank Crowther, December, 1983.

The Legislative Imperative for School Library Media Programs

Thomas Hart

In the United States, only twelve to fourteen states have consistent legislative programs with a legislative lobbyist. It is imperative that more states become involved in legislative activity. Leaders of state school library media organizations must make their legislation committee a top priority. Look at your organization's budget! What areas receive the most attention? Usually they are: (1) the state journal, (2) administration costs, or (3) convention planning costs. How can the cycle be broken?

FIRST YEAR

1. Appoint a chairperson of the legislation committee who is near or in the capitol. Make an appointment long term, so consistency can be developed;

2. Appoint a legislation committee which is representative of the major concerns in your state organization and who have political acumen and contacts;

3. Provide a budget for the legislative chairperson to hold legislative workshops and three legislative committee meetings to develop the goals and objectives of the committee;

4. Develop a network of politically aware members who can be relied upon to contact other members to persuade key legislators.

SECOND YEAR

1. Develop a platform of concerns in priority order, which can have a possibility of being accomplished. Don't attempt areas which are not possible to change with a fledgling organization,

2. Encourage network members to visit key legislators and report their discussions.

3. Hire a part-time lobbyist who has had previous legislative experience;

4. Introduce one bill of primary concern which can be the focal point for committee action.

THIRD YEAR AND BEYOND

1. Keep developing a new platform each year, changing priorities with the emphasis on state government;

2. Maintain an active network, constantly bringing in new members;

3. Develop new avenues of contact.

CHRONICLE OF A SUCCESSFUL LEGISLATIVE PROGRAM

In the mid 1950s the wife of a powerful legislator in the state of Florida convinced him to introduce a bill concerning school library programs. A major component of that bill was the definition of a program and a statement that school librarians were instructional personnel like all other teachers. The bill also emphasized that there should be one librarian for every 500 students per school. Even though this bill was never funded, the concept became a part of *Florida Standards*. In fact, by the mid-1960s it was reported that there was one librarian per 518 students. When the initial legislation was passed, a strong and persistent director of school libraries at the Florida Department of Education provided further impetus toward reaching the standards proposed in the law. After this initial success, there was not a strong legislative effort until 1975.

During the early 1970s state standards for schools were eliminated, because of the new emphasis on "school-based management." Also, three media-related organizations, Florida School Librarians Association (FSLA), Florida Audio Visual Association (FAVA), and Florida Association for Educational Television (FAETV), were in the process of merging and were not able, at that time, to mount a strong legislative activity. In 1975, Shirley Aaron was asked to re-establish the legislative network.

ESTABLISHING A NETWORK

With the assistance of a strong influential legislative committee, a network of fourteen regions in the state was established. Individuals with political contacts were asked to serve. The state was divided into three areas to hold training workshops. Each of the fourteen regional contacts was asked to select a legislative contact in the county school district in their region (Florida has sixty-seven school districts, one for each county). The agenda at the workshops included:

1. The process for introducing legislation in the Florida Legislature.

2. Methods for making appointments with legislators:

   • Call their offices when they are in their home districts

   • Set a time when you can talk to the legislator in person

   • Talk with the chief aide if the legislator is not available

   • Send a report to the legislative committee chairperson

3. Make-up of the visiting team:

   • Usually three; one spokesperson and two "nodders" for moral support

   • An influential superintendent, principal and/or teacher who is a strong supporter of school library media programs

4. Focus of the discussion with legislators:

   • Know enough about the special interests of the legislator, to tailor the requests in their same framework of reference

   • Have statistics to back up concerns

   • If you don't know the answers to their questions, admit it and then suggest that you will obtain the information in a timely fashion

5. How to become active in political campaigns

6. Questions and discussion

DEVELOPING A TELEPHONE TREE

After the legislative committee developed the "legislative platform," the network contacts were appointed in fourteen regions, and county contacts were appointed for most school districts, then it was time to introduce the first bill in the legislature. The legislative committee decided to introduce a bill to update terminology in the existing state laws and to establish a new section of programs to be required in all schools. These programs included skills instruction, instructional design, management, and production services. Key legislators were targeted to introduce and sign on to the bill. Dr. Aaron enlisted faculty colleagues to visit legislators and union leaders in Tallahassee. A key senator, chair of the Senate Education Committee, was coerced into introducing the bill in the Senate. (The chair of the House Education Committee could not be persuaded to introduce the bill.) The first year, the Senate passed the bill, but the house didn't; the second year the house passed the bill, but it was defeated in the Senate.

These two years of defeats caused the legislative committee to look at different ways of operating. As with most lawmakers, the Florida Legislature usually waits until the last few weeks to make important decisions, and a few key legislators really control what bills make it to the floor for a vote. We decided to establish a "telephone tree" to make contacts in the four to six regions and identify county contacts; the county contacts identified four to six people able to respond quickly. For example, we called one regional contact, because the legislator in her area was not willing to speak for our bill on the floor. She called six contacts and they each called six to eight contacts. We were able to jam the senator's phone lines to the point that he asked our lobbyist to "call off the horses." He was instantly reminded of the "power" of a unified and organized group of school library media specialists.

Telephone Trees are necessary when early instant communication is needed with legislators. They require dedicated library media specialists to keep them operational, so they can be used at strategic times.

HIRE A LOBBYIST

It took three years to pass our original law and it finally passed because of the untiring efforts of the lobbyist hired by the Florida Association for Media in Education (FAME). I had become the new chair of the FAME legislation committee, but Dr. Aaron had already laid the groundwork for hiring a lobbyist. Fortunately, one of the recent graduates of the School of Library and Information Studies at Florida State University was the spouse of a prominent lobbyist for insurance interests. She wanted to work part-time, had no lobbying experience, but had many legislative contacts through her husband. We convinced her that she could do it, and Mary Margaret Rogers took the job in 1977.

Originally our lobbyist's responsibilities were just during the three month legislative session, but they have branched out to include helping set up the network, planning for legislative workshops at the FAME annual conference, and at other times as needed. She also coordinates visits with key legislators and goes with FAME members in the region who need encouragement.

Without a lobbyist, FAME's legislative program would begin to deteriorate. It takes a unique person to thrive on the endless committee meetings and machinations of the legislature.

ESTABLISHING A LEGISLATIVE AWARD

With the success of our legislative program came the responsibility to keep our visibility at a high level within FAME and the legislature. Six years ago we initiated an award for the legislator who had assisted us the most during the previous year. The first recipient was the senator who introduced our first bill. Every attempt has been made to create a dynamic atmosphere for the award program.

The major elements are:

• The legislative general session is one of three general sessions during the FAME's annual three day conference.

• The auditorium is decorated in red, white, and blue, with placards on sticks to identify the fourteen regions in the state.

- Members are seated by regions.

- The regions representing the honored legislators bring them into the auditorium while the audience sings patriotic songs.

- We sometimes share slide-tapes or videotapes produced by local school districts to help with their lobbying efforts.

- The platform is discussed in detail while the honored legislator listens.

- The legislator speaks and responds to questions from the audience.

- Contributions from county school library media associations are recognized.

The legislative award has become so significant, that a few years ago, one of the honorees came from Jacksonville, Florida, and the convention was held in Orlando, Florida. It was a foggy morning so his first flight was cancelled, he then attempted two other flights before he was successful, arriving at the end of the program. Nevertheless he made every effort to be present.

REJUVENATING THE NETWORK

Florida has had a significant legislative program for 12 years without interruption. About every four years our lobbyist and legislative chairperson plan workshops to encourage new participants in the network. These workshops include elements from the original sessions, but we also spend time sharing new techniques from experienced regional participants. We also share slide/tape and video productions which they might possibly use in their legislative visits.

THE RESULTS?

We have not always been successful in obtaining our legislative goals, but because of the efforts of a few persistent FAME members, most library media programs enjoy the fruits of these efforts. What are the results of this twelve-year program?

- A revised law which has implications for state audits that have expanded library media programs state-wide

- Increased and consistent funding for Instructional Television Grants and an expanded video distribution program

- An average state grant of $3,000 per school to upgrade A-V equipment and/or library media collections during the past 7 years

- A strong voice for intellectual freedom

- Increased and consistent funding for community colleges

- Increased and consistent funding for universities

- Participation in merit pay over the objections of teachers' unions

- Major role in developing career ladder programs

- Persuaded the legislature to fund a networking study which has added a staff member to the library media section of the Florida Department of Education

- Ensured that school library media specialists are represented on state study commissions and state boards

In conclusion, it is interesting to note that for the first time in Florida, the governor's wife is a library media specialist. Our state cabinet meets once a month as the state board of education. In early February (the new governor's first meeting) they were discussing "criteria of excellence" (common criteria among schools where students' achievement scores had increased). The Governor asked, "Why weren't there any criteria for library media programs?" For the first time in recent history, the commissioner of education's staff scurried around to see what criteria should be included.

The new commissioner of education has been a strong supporter of school library media programs when she was a state senator. She even held her swearing-in ceremony in a local school library media center.

Even though we have lost some of our "friends" in the legislature, things look bright for the future. We will continue to spread the message to the next generation of legislators with a consistent and well funded legislative program!

Professional Lobbyist and Volunteer Professionals: A Formidable Force for Advocacy

Mary Margaret Rogers

On Friday, August 30, 1985, Hurricane Elena wove her erratic path back and forth over the Gulf of Mexico, alternately threatening the west coast, then the north coastal area of Florida. Braving the elements and calling on lady luck, members of the legislation committee of the Florida Association for Media in Education, Inc. (FAME) gathered in Tallahassee, Florida's capital city, to evaluate needs and set priorities for the 1985-86 legislative platform. This committee must evaluate and compile input from school-based library media specialists, supervisory personnel, school library educators, any and all FAME members throughout the state, into a statement of library media priorities in need of legislative remedy.

The committee worked diligently all day, stopping only for lunch and a noon hurricane advisory. A rough draft platform was completed in time for two members to catch the last plane headed south out of Tallahassee for several days to come.

Dr. Thomas Hart, legislation committee chair, and the FAME lobbyist smoothed the rough draft into a full fledged legislative platform presented to FAME members at the annual conference, September 26-29. With an average attendance of 1,000, this conference offers a yearly opportunity for the professional lobbyist to interact with association members, the potential volunteers who visit their legislators at home. Contacts were established and cultivated. A concurrent session used an outside lobbyist as well as the FAME lobbyist to motivate and train volunteers to visit and persuade legislators. Those members attending this session signed their names and addresses on a sheet of paper which became a valuable resource list for the lobbyist and legislation committee to use in developing the FAME Network for 1985-86.

A large, well-attended General Session was staged along the lines of a political rally, with singing, presentation of our platform and most importantly, FAME's annual award to a Legislator who has been an outstanding supporter of school library media programs. House of Representatives Appropriations Committee Chair Sam Bell, Daytona Beach, Florida, received the 1985 FAME award. Rep. Bell went home with first-hand knowledge of our enthusiastic professional association and its legislative platform for the upcoming 1986 legislative session. He also carried away an impressive plaque for the wall in his office, a frequent reminder of school library media needs. FAME members went home with first-hand knowledge of another legislative leader, his ideas for our professional improvement and an admonishment to support tax increases to pay for our legislative platform.

THE NETWORK

A network of fifteen volunteer contacts coordinates the local legislative efforts of the association. These contacts, in turn, establish a local network of FAME members to educate their local Legislators to library media needs. To accomplish passage of legislation meeting those identified needs, volunteers have three crucial tasks: pre-session visits, quick action calls or letters during the session, and post-session thank you's.

The FAME legislation chair/lobbyist team went to work on soliciting the 1985-86 fifteen volunteers. Many contacts continued from previous years and a few from large metropolitan areas were assigned by local association elections. The remaining vacancies were filled by November and the 1985-86 FAME legislative network was in place, ready, willing and able to solicit representatives' and senators' commitments of support for the FAME platform.

Packets of information and instructions, compiled by the lobbyist, were mailed to network contacts. Each contained an assignment sheet designating priority order for visits to be made. Visit and convince the leadership of each house first, including our conference speaker, Rep. Bell; next visit other key chairpersons and committee members; finally, visit all remaining legislators. They may be key next year or the next.

The network went to work. All over Florida, individual legislators were personally apprised of school library media program needs and FAME's proposed solutions. They were educated by their local library media specialists, friends, neighbors and most importantly, voters—their constituents. The great majority of representatives and senators agreed to help "as much as I can." This means, when dollars are needed, we will try to squeeze a share for your programs.

The first plank of the 1985-86 platform was a big ticket request to continue and increase a state categorical appropriation for materials and equipment in Florida schools. Another plank was a small ticket request for a totally new $50,000 to fund a networking study. New programs of any kind, even inexpensive ones, are very hard to accomplish in a legislative budget bill. The categorical dollars for materials were crucial to library media programs and our advocates must do nothing to jeopardize an increase in those funds. Diversion of these dollars to study networking was totally unacceptable to FAME, but a common response from many legislators upon hearing both proposals in our platform.

Among the many volunteers working for the FAME platform were Hillsborough County school library media specialists who visited Senator Betty Castor, chairperson of the Senate Appropriations sub-committee for Education, and the key senator for educational funding issues. Three Leon County library media specialists met with Representative Herb Morgan, past Appropriations chair, present Rules Committee chair, and a powerful representative for educational funding. Both Sen. Castor and Rep. Morgan agreed to support our platform items including new funds for the networking study. Both delegations notified the lobbyist of these commitments.

THE PROCESS

The legislative session began April 8, 1986, and within the week, budget hearing became earnest. Appropriations committees spend many hours hearing testimony, discussing budget requests and speculating where to find the dollars needed to fund even bare bones increases. However, when the time comes for the committee to finalize its proposed budget, it moves with lightning speed—a word here, a figure on the papers there, or a quick motion and line items are set. The House and Senate budget proposals are committed to a bill overnight! Once a bill, the budget is a moving train; it is relatively easy to throw a line item off the train, but hard to catch up and add one on to it. The categorical funds for materials were on the budget, but the $50,000 networking study was still waiting at the station.

Wednesday afternoon in mid-May, 1 p.m.: The House appropriations sub-committees met and let it be known their final proposals would be voted out of committee at 8 a.m. Thursday morning. The networking study dollars must be there. Because it was a new program it required a motion from a committee member. Remember Committee Member Morgan's commitment to the Tallahassee library media specialists? Now was the time to remind him to act on it, and FAME's professional lobbyist did just that. Before the afternoon floor session was adjourned, she was waiting in line in Rep. Morgan's office for five minutes with him. At least the boredom of two-and-one-half hours of waiting was broken by visiting among the many other lobbyists there. Finally, at 6:15 p.m., Rep. Morgan emerged from his inner sanctum and said, "Walk with me, Mary Margaret. You have the time it takes to get to the Speaker's office?" (Around the corner and down the hall took two minutes at the most!) "Mr. Morgan, remember last February when you committed to Mrs. Freeman and Mrs. Sewell to support $50,000 for a school library networking study?" Mr. Morgan responded, "Yes I do, and if you'll put exactly what I need to do in a note, have it for me as we begin our meeting in the morning, I'll see to it." He did! After additional work with Rep. Morgan and the committee staff, the house appropriations bill contained a simple, but meaningful line item, "$50,000—Networking Study."

But the House budget is only half the story. The $50,000 must be in the senate appropriations bill also, to give security for inclusion in the final legislative appropriations bill.

The Senate budget committees met the next day to finalize their bills. The story is the same but a different place and people. The FAME lobbyist waited in line with many other lobbyists in Senate Appropriations sub-committee for education chairperson Castor's office. A quick reminder of Ms. Zack's and Ms. Hudson's visit in Tampa, and she had her

aide insert proviso language setting aside dollars from a statewide information network to cover our library media program networking study. We were in both Senate and House bills but in different ways and at differing dollar amounts.

The House and Senate must compromise and agree on a final appropriations bill. The lobbyists monitoring this process describe it yearly as hours of boredom punctuated by moments of sheer terror. The big ticket materials dollars were protected and maximized, and the best possible position was acquired for the networking study. The lobbyist worked with Senate committee staff to persuade them to concur with the cleaner House line item proposal. They were convinced. The final appropriations bill of the 1986 legislative session, signed by a supportive and well-lobbied governor, addressed two of the Florida Association for Media in Education's Platform requests. Neither volunteers nor the lobbyist could have done the job alone, but together, complementing each other, FAME won!

Voila! FAME's strategies paid off again. Voters solicited the legislator's support and got a commitment; then a professional lobbyist followed through in the capitol to effect a winning position for school library media programs.

THE KEY

Crucial elements of this formula for volunteer and professional cooperation are:

- Appointed representatives from the volunteer force, the legislation committee, are charged with creating a platform to address common needs of Florida school library media programs. A platform must come from real and pressing needs and never be created narrowly or superficially. This gives it strong support from the majority of association members. The professional lobbyist may advise committee members on possible legislative solutions to meet the identified needs.

- The paid lobbyist educates and inspires the general membership to participate in visits to individual legislators as well as being professionally politic in general.

- Volunteers are organized through a network of fifteen state leaders who take responsibility for carrying out the state plan at the local level. Since library media advocates do not have political clout generated by money, these local voters become the powerful clout on which we rely.

- The lobbyist uses expertise and a thorough knowledge of the political process and people to assign priorities to the volunteers for visiting legislators. Area network contacts are advised which legislators are in key positions of leadership or are of crucial concern and power concerning our issues.

- Volunteers visit or otherwise contact legislators and report the results of these visits to the lobbyist. Conversely, the lobbyist follows up on assignments with the network contacts if no reports have been made.

Volunteers also identify the lobbyist to legislators as their representative in Tallahassee.

- The lobbyist assumes the responsibility for passage of the proposed legislation, but may call on the volunteer force during the session to reinforce points made previously.

- Protecting the overall interests of school library media programs is also the responsibility of a lobbyist. If issues arise adversely affecting our interests, volunteers may be called upon for quick response to help kill bad legislation. This only works if the groundwork was laid by personal contact prior to the session.

- Both lobbyist and volunteers follow through with thank you letters and phone calls to all legislators who helped pass our legislation. Thank you's help perpetuate good will for us and pave the way for the cycle to begin again for the next year.

A professional lobbyist in the capitol cannot carry the ball alone without constituent support. As volunteers, on the job media professionals cannot follow through with attention to details that are crucial to passing legislation. Library media advocates generally do not have the political clout generated by money. They do have voter clout. Legislators listen to constituents, especially when they bring needs of public school students to them. Combine the expertise of a good professional lobbyist in the actual legislative arena (the capitol) with the powerful influence of voters supporting improved education for all students and you have a formidable force moving for improved school library media programs.

How to Lobby by Letter, by Phone, in Person

LOBBY ...

NOUN: A waiting room

VERB: To try to influence legislators to vote in a certain way

We've been in the waiting room too long! Let's use our influence to make things happen!

DEVELOP A PLAN

1. **Enlist support** of all individuals or groups involved in, or affected by, the issue(s).

2. **Organize** a meeting of representatives of these groups.

3. At the meeting decide on the basic issue or issues involved. **Focus attention** on 2 or 3 issues. Too many issues discussed at one time limit effectiveness.

4. **Involve influential people** from your community in your campaign—councillors, the mayor, prominent citizens.

5. **Study different methods** of lobbying.

DECIDE THE METHODS

1. **Letter Lobby:** numbers count
   - Ask every member to get a friend of every organization to write a letter.
   - Ask each member to get a friend to write a letter.
   - Write directly to the politician(s) or head of the corporation you wish to influence.
   - Prepare a sample letter.
   - Be brief, to the point. State what is wrong and what you would like to see done to remedy it.

2. **Phone lobby:** Again, numbers count.
   - Ask every member of every organization to phone; ask each member to get a friend to phone.
   - If you can, speak to the politician(s) or head of corporation. If you are "screened," leave a definite message, stating your views briefly. Don't ramble.

3. **Personal lobby:** Legislature, parliament or corporation.

This material adapted from "Facing Down the Man" by Nancy Henley and used with the permission of the Canadian Advisory Council on the Status of Women.

- Phone for an appointment.
- Mention the topics you would like to discuss.
- Have a copy of material you are presenting to leave with the politician (president).
- Be prepared to provide background information—be informed.
- Keep to the points you wish to discuss—don't be sidetracked.

4. **Submission of a brief:** In person, if possible.
   - Select members to prepare and present the brief.
   - Canvass members of groups for ideas or resource material.
   - Submit the brief to all parties who can wield influence in your favour.

5. **A press conference** will publicize your concern.

6. **Establish a continuing contact** in each of the media. Provide your contact with background information so that your position will be understood. Keep the contact informed.

DEFINE THE TARGET

1. **Legislators** respond to influence if it will affect their prospects for re-election. Lobbying techniques must reflect your ability to influence the vote.

2. **Corporations** respond to influence if it will affect their profit statements. Publicize your campaign to influence a corporation.

MONITORING—HOW TO RUN AN OBSERVER CORPS

1. You are not finished with your lobbying process until concrete action has been taken on your issue.

2. **Legislation lobbying**
   - Arrange to have someone attend sessions of the legislature to listen to debate.
   - Try to establish a contact within each party who will let you know when they plan to speak to your bill.
   - Attend the committee hearings pertinent to your bill.
   - Keep notes of the proceedings. Be prepared to recommend to the group you represent, further action required.
   - Be sure that the legislators know that you are watching them and listening to them.

- Write letters of thanks or approval when appropriate. Letters are the politicians' bread and butter.

CORPORATION LOBBYING

1. Organize a letter lobby.

2. Write a personal letter to the president of the company asking for a report on action taken on your previous requests.

3. Make an appointment for a delegation to see the president—Ask for a report on actions taken.

4. Write letters of thanks or approval when appropriate.

NEGOTIATION TECHNIQUES

In organizing for social change, individuals and groups must meet with the person who has the power to make decisions. Very often this person has had years of experience in handling confrontation situations. Following are some tips to assist groups pushing for social change in dealing with meetings.

1. Use the "common problem" approach. You are recognizing a problem and getting together in an attempt to solve it.

2. Your case must be strong enough to stand on its own merit. For example, the United Nations Charter on Human Rights has been signed by Canada. Therefore all groups in Canada should promote and agree to its terms.

3. Present a whole document, embodying all items on which you are seeking agreement. Don't add on to the initial package. Establish your priorities beforehand, and know which items you are prepared to debate.

4. Be aware of their priorities. Some items may be easy or hard for them to provide. You can give up one hard item to obtain three or four of your items.

5. Establish regular meetings with the group. You can then introduce contentious issues gradually—prepare a mindset towards controversial innovations.

6. Learn to identify the leading personalities of the group with which you are dealing. Direct your persuasion toward these dominant personalities.

7. Never lose your sense of humour. Disregard personal remarks. Lighten the situation whenever possible.

8. Above all—be prepared. Know costs of what you are requesting and don't gloss them over. Justify them but don't cover up.

9. Select your best qualified and most experienced people to speak for you, regardless of their position in the group.

10. Anticipate the arguments of the group and be prepared to refute them.

11. Simplify your proposals.

12. Be flexible. Be sensitive to the reactions of your audience. Adapt your arguments to these reactions.

The Trustee as School Library Advocate

Ken Haycock

Education is a community concern. Governments have legislative authority for education but it is the local involvement of citizens in each community that gives public education its heart.

The members of the board of school trustees of each school district are elected by the residents to govern its public education in a progressive, farsighted, educationally sound, and economically-feasible manner. While only a board has legal authority to implement policy, a single trustee can and does have the opportunity to become knowledgeable about, and an advocate for, library resource centers and teacher-librarians in our schools on an individual basis.

HOW CAN TRUSTEES BE EFFECTIVE SCHOOL LIBRARY ADVOCATES?

Trustees are leaders in the community. They indicate support for school library programs when they attend school library events and classes planned and team-taught by classroom teachers and teacher-librarians. Trustees can make themselves knowledgeable about school libraries in each school, the program being offered, and the adequacy of support in terms of personnel, materials, equipment and facilities to support resource-based teaching and learning. It is reasonable to expect that each school district has a policy statement on school libraries in education, and if no such policy exists, any trustee can propose one.

Trustees can also act as a check to see that standards recommended by the state government and school district for school libraries are carried out in elementary and secondary schools. Both allocation of time and appropriate staff selection to make school library programs effective should be priorities in each district along with a fair share of equipment and supply budgets. Once these programs are in place, it is reasonable to expect that program evaluations are conducted to ensure ongoing quality. The results of these evaluations should be reported to the board.

Trustees often have the ability and the opportunity to communicate to the media, and can publicize the many wonderful learning opportunities and achievements arising from instruction through teacher and teacher-librarian cooperation

and co-curricular activities. Trustees help just by attending events and seeing work that is being done. In many cases, the teachers and teacher-librarian are planning together and the students are involved in guided independent work before school, at noon breaks and after school, after everyone else has gone home. They are encouraged by even a simple, "Well done!" from trustees whom they view as educational policy leaders.

Perhaps board meetings would be more interesting with a brief presentation on a student assignment or project which resulted from good school libraries. District offices or board rooms may be a good location for a display of student work. Trustees may be able to rally community support for materials and volunteer assistance so that the teacher-librarian can leave fund-raising and clerical/technical routine to someone else, and concentrate on teaching. In brief, the opportunities to help give children access to quality school library experiences are unlimited—any active involvement will help.

WHAT KIND OF TRUSTEE CAN BE A SCHOOL LIBRARY ADVOCATE?

The kind of trustee who can improve school library education is the one who is interested and committed. Once a person accepts the value of good library resource centers as part of the basic program and necessary on an equal basis with other instructional services, he or she just needs to be persistent. The district policy will outline the aim of the program, the role and qualifications of teacher-librarians, criteria and procedures for the selection of materials and handling complaints and it will insist on flexibly scheduled resource centers after teacher/teacher-librarian planning to prevent teacher-librarians being misused to provide spare periods for classroom teachers; the goals and learning outcomes are defined; and program evaluation procedures should be in place.

A trustee who is willing to visit and support school libraries; a trustee who will ask appropriate questions and persist until satisfactory answers are given; and a trustee who values the development of skills to process and use information and pursue lifelong learning will be successful as an advocate.

TRUSTEE ACTION PROGRAM FOR SCHOOL LIBRARIES

Here are some suggestions for actions a trustee, or group of trustees, can take to support opportunities for young people to learn through the resources and services of a good school library. All of them will have an effect — doing some of them will have an effect. Even one will likely make the situation for school libraries better than it is at present — the key is action!

ACTION IDEAS:

- Investigate whether your district has a policy which guarantees equal opportunity for students to use school libraries in each school. If no policy exists, institute one. Sample policies are available through both school library associations and trustee associations.

- Request from administration a statement about the status of school library standards for personnel and resources and the effectiveness of their use.

- Request a program assessment of school library programs so decisions can be made about changes and improvements based on up-to-date data.

- Ask for information about the number of elementary teacher-librarians and secondary teacher-librarians on staff and the number of teachers they work with; staffing patterns should reflect the number of teachers to plan with as well as the number of students in the school.

- Compare allocations on school library materials with allocations in other curricular areas.

- Inquire regarding the extent to which cooperatively planned and taught school library programs are restricted by the initiative of the principal and individual teacher; support an in-depth staff development program to encourage effective school library use.

- Request an assessment of school library facilities and equipment in each school and the impact on the instructional program of any identified deficiencies.

- Ask for presentations on each area of the curriculum using school library resources and services and at each level — 15 minutes per board meeting bimonthly could be devoted to an explanation or demonstration of school library learning.

- Develop a relationship with municipal or community library people with a view to advocating better libraries for everyone so that roles can be better defined and resources can be better shared.

- Ask to have a specific administrator appointed as the person responsible for supervising and developing school library programs in your district. This should be a school library supervisor who has special knowledge and training, not only in managing a district resource center but in building networks of libraries, advocating effective use and leading in-service sessions on cooperative program planning and teaching, including the roles of the district, principal and teacher. Professional associations and departments of education have statements on the role and responsibilities of school library supervisors.

- Attend school library programs in schools and encourage other trustees to attend. Volunteer to open these events and welcome parents as well as acknowledging the work done by the teacher and students.

- Make awareness of, and sensitivity to, school library programs an integral part of the criteria for the selection and appointment of school and district administrators. These criteria should also be applied to the assessment of these educational leaders.

- Encourage your administration to see that trained teacher-librarians are hired in numbers sufficient to meet the curricular needs for all students.

- Encourage professional development to help administrators, teachers and teacher-librarians remain aware of their roles in fostering the school library resource center in the curriculum, in developing cooperatively planned and taught programs, in new methodology, and current trends.

Above all, remember that the key is action. A trustee can make a qualitative difference in school library programs for the children in the district. Opportunities to learn through school libraries enrich the child, and the school library is part of the educational right of every child. Protecting that right is part of the trust.

Twenty Ways to Invite School Board Members

Dean Fink

1. **No surprises:** School board members hate surprises. They need to be aware of your successes and difficulties, real or anticipated. Most school board members support schools and can contribute to your success if they are treated as able, worthwhile, and responsible people by school staff.

2. **Invite school board members to share your celebrations:** Always acknowledge their presence. They should be front and center at your special programs as well as at school graduation, parents' meetings, sports and musical activities. They tend to hear the negative, so let them share the positive.

3. **Keep your communication free of jargon:** School board members are partners, not "the enemy." It's best to work together towards the same goal—that is, to improve schooling for all children. Jargon is often perceived as a putdown by the non-professional.

4. **Keep your reports brief:** Say what you mean, mean what you say. School board members must read a great deal to make informed decisions. Respect their time by not contributing to their information overload.

5. **Include school board members in key committees:** School board members can be your eyes and ears to the community. Involvement in goal setting and policy committees allows them to contribute their unique perspective, while providing them with an informed view of the dynamics of a school and its resource center.

6. **Plan an orientation program for new trustees:** A well-planned, informative orientation helps school board members to feel a part of the team. They can function more effectively and feel like a contributing partner right from the beginning. Why not have a graduation cake and gag gifts to celebrate the end of orientation?

7. **Take a school board member to lunch:** Good relationships begin over a cup of coffee and a bowl of soup.

8. **Give prompt service:** School board members are important to the success of our schools. Treat their requests and inquiries seriously. If a parental concern is referred to you by a school board member act promptly and report your actions.

9. **Make their job easier:** Can you arrange secretarial help? Can you provide information? Are there tasks which you can do which help them to succeed? Give them your thoughts on board agenda items.

10. **Share the limelight:** Most school board members are elected. Help them to be re-elected by arranging for media exposure or directing reporters to solicit their views. Acknowledge the role of the school board at important occasions. Introduce them to the staff and your schools' parents. If things go wrong, accept the blame, don't dump on the Board. School board members want to know they impact on education.

11. **Make sure school board members feel comfortable to visit your school and resource center:** Ensure that they meet the staff, know the building and feel at ease to drop in.

12. **Encourage school board members' participation in professional development activities:** To build trusting relationships and to make school board members feel like part of the team, encourage them to listen to topical speakers, participate in workshops or attend conferences. An informed school board member is a powerful ally.

13. **Encourage school board members' direct involvement with students:** Most school board members genuinely want what is best for students. Provide opportunities for direct involvement. Invite them to chaperone, participate in a canoe trip, speak to a class on an area of expertise, lead a tour, assist in an assembly, give out awards, have lunch with students.

14. **Don't embarrass a school board member through unprofessional behavior:** School board members sometimes get caught between their responsibility to the public and loyalty to staff. You can keep them out of this dilemma by acting in a professional manner at all times. Use school board money wisely since they are responsible to the public.

15. **Seek their advice:** Test their views on issues which affect the school. Ask to involve them in your program evaluation.

16. **Speak in positive terms about school board members:** School boards must constantly weigh three policy decisions when they vote on any issue: equity, quality and efficiency. It's a tough job to weigh these often competing pressures and in a public forum be accountable. Speak positively about your school board members even when you don't approve of their decisions. The self-fulfilling prophecy even works in board rooms.

17. **Send a letter of appreciation:** School board members need invitations and get few. They hear from the displeased or distressed but seldom receive the accolades they often deserve. Balance the equation by a note or a card to express appreciation.

18. **Invite school board members to speak to your staff:** This is an excellent way to give recognition to your school board member, while helping your colleagues to see the political side of the educational enterprise.

19. **Attend board meetings:** Support your school board members by your presence. Your attendance helps you to understand issues from the board's point of view. Hearsay and media reports are poor substitutes for firsthand information.

20. **Take your school board member to exemplary schools or classrooms:** The shared experience of pursuing excellence will help cement a relationship.

How to Get Your Legislator's Ear

Charles Parr

The first, and most important thing to know and remember about your legislative representatives is that they are not much different from you. They want to do the right thing. While your professional life may revolve around the library, the legislator's attention is split among widely divergent matters. It would not be unusual to deal in one day with royal oil contracts, state medical insurance, criminal code changes, forestry, and teacher retirement. You have to take the initiative to see that library needs are not lost in the shuffle.

Civic-minded and well-informed citizens will know their representatives in the Senate and in the House. Do you know them personally? You can and you should know at least some of them well. If you have not met your lawmakers, get in touch with someone politically active and arrange to meet them when they are in town.

During election campaigns try to meet all major candidates. You never know who will win and represent you. Besides, the one who loses may win in two years. A word of warning about taking sides publicly: if your candidate wins it may help, but if the opponent is the one sworn in, you will have more trouble getting any attention.

Personal contact, the best way to get your message across, is not always possible. Next is a well-written, brief letter (typed if possible) explaining clearly what you want and why. Do not expect your legislator to be familiar with all details of a problem but, if you have already given them in a personal meeting, tactfully mention that you have. Do not use technical terms or in-house jargon; use language understandable by an intelligent layperson. Finally, be courteous. Legislators already get enough ill-tempered letters.

A busy legislator spends little time in the office. Phone calls will probably not reach him or her directly, but you may develop a relationship with a staff member whom you can reach by phone. Telegrams do not serve much useful purpose because they are too short and a favored vehicle for pressure groups.

Visits to the capital may be expensive and probably will not justify the cost. If you are going while the legislature is in session, write first and ask for an appointment with your legislators. It is fairly certain one will be squeezed in for you although it may be at an odd time.

Now, as to the content of your verbal or written message, remember your legislator wants to do right. You have to show what you propose is right. Marshal your facts in advance and present them in an organized way. Keep to the main points with fact sheets showing details. Do not oversell your case.

If pictures are appropriate, use them. If not, a brief, well-painted word picture, or a human interest feature, can make a point. Legislators are more interested in human beings than in statistics.

Finally, the most important work is done in committees. Your legislator may not be on the committee which handles your interest. In this case ask for advice about contacting the committee. You will probably get the names of committee members most likely to give you a favorable hearing.

Know your legislators. Do not be timid. You hired your legislators and they are there to work for you and your district.

Good Luck!

School Libraries — A Rationale

Alberta Learning Resources Council

INTRODUCTION

The Learning Resources Council of the Alberta Teachers' Association was challenged to prepare a brief but clear rationale for school libraries. Their objective was to explain the critical function of school library programs in preparing students to become lifelong learners who are able to cope with change, and who are able to fulfill their roles in society, both now and in the future. Contributors to this paper were Bev Anderson and Barry Eshpeter of Calgary, Kay Iseke of St. Albert and Sheila Pritchard and Dianne Oberg of Edmonton.

FUTURE

Our society is an information society — characterized by rapidly advancing technology and overwhelming change. Information available is now doubling every eight to ten years.

TECHNOLOGY

How should schools prepare students for an increasingly uncertain future? This issue is raised frequently by concerned parents, by educators, and by the media.

CHANGES

This creates serious problems for information users. For example, students need to learn how to separate the meaningful and useful from the irrelevant. The skills of "learning how to learn," the skills of lifelong learning, are necessary to prepare them to cope with change.

DEMOCRACY

This preparation for life should be regarded as fundamental. Our commitment to a free and open society is dependent upon having citizens who are able to acquire and analyze information in order to make independent decisions. As the pervasiveness of electronic media increases, the individual's skill for analyzing information becomes more critical.

BIAS

Students must learn to detect bias, to evaluate information sources, to consider both sides of an issue. They must practice these skills throughout their education if they are to participate effectively as adults in our society.

LEARNING STYLES

Students practice these skills when they are taught using a wide variety of materials in a wide variety of ways. As well, the diverse needs and learning styles of individual students are best met when this approach to education is chosen. Not all of us learn best from the printed page; for some of us, other formats provide better ways to learn.

GIFTED/SPECIAL

This is true of all students, not only the gifted or special education student. The teacher and the textbook, once considered adequate sources of information, are no longer sufficient.

DEFICIENCY

Are Alberta students being prepared for an effective role in their society? Unfortunately, many students in this province are denied the opportunity to develop the skills necessary to participate fully in their society.

EFFECTIVE PROGRAMS

There are vast differences in the levels of school library development in Alberta. In some school districts, school libraries are seen as a priority. In such areas, students can select from a wide range of learning resources. They are instructed in locating and using information by professional educators. Teachers and teacher-librarians co-operatively develop lesson plans, and learning activities for their students.

LACK STAFF/NO SERVICES

In some districts, although facilities and basic resources appear to be in place, the staff or time needed to plan learning activities is not provided. In other districts, no library services or programs exist.

GOAL OF SCHOOLING

The third goal of schooling, as defined by the Alberta government in 1979, states that

> programs and activities shall be planned, taught, and evaluated ... in order that students:
> — develop the learning skills of finding, organizing, analyzing, and applying information in a constructive and objective manner.

LIBRARIES ESSENTIAL

School libraries are essential in ensuring that students "learn to learn." Students who have not had access to quality school library programs lack adequate skills to effectively use public and academic libraries and other information sources important for their work and for their personal lives. A viable school library program should be available to every student in Alberta.

CRUCIAL TIME

This is a crucial time in the development of school library services in Alberta. There are indications that students are graduating from school now without skills for either post-secondary education or lifelong learning.

ACTION

Action on this issue must begin now.

ELECTIONS

Although provincial leadership is critical, decisions regarding staffing and funding libraries are made at district and school levels. Municipal and school board officials' positions greatly affect the quality of education.

Part 4
THE CONCLUSION

Confidence in the product...
Commitment to excellence and growth...
Strategies to effect change...
What more can one say?

HANG TOGETHER OR

HANG SEPARATELY:

PROGRAM ADVOCACY

AND POWER

Commitments to Quality...

Ken Haycock

Several years ago, a major school board eliminated more than half of the district resource centre staff including all six professional positions except the coordinator. In that same year (1983), another large district amalgamated two resource divisions with a resulting reduction in staff and increased vulnerability in the future. School-based budgets and staff are still being reduced and even eliminated in many districts due to mandated cutbacks from ministries of education. Add to this the loss of faculty positions in school librarianship in some faculties of library science and education, and the situation starts to appear grim.

At the same time, however, there is reason to be "cautiously optimistic." Some districts have maintained and even strengthened school library services, as districts made their cuts in programs with a lower priority than library services. Several districts both in and outside of Ontario are developing systematic and comprehensive implementation strategies. And existing programs for education for school librarianship are being appraised and improved through internal and external review. Perhaps a new foundation is being laid for a better thrust for school librarianship.

Quite apart from the obvious and well-developed programs of advocacy, the supportive boards seem to have a well-stated or at least well-understood "mission statement." In other words, not only teacher-librarians, but others in the district as well, can articulate a common aim for the school library program, and usually in as precise terms as one sentence. In critical times it is urgent that all district staff and teacher-librarians be able to state strongly, in sound educational terms, the purpose of the investment in resource centres as an essential service.

The aim of these programs focuses on purpose, not on activities. This is a more important point than might first appear. The underlying premise of the library program is that it is a cooperatively planned and taught program, thus objectives may be achieved by principals, teachers and/or teacher-librarians, working together or independently. For example, book talks, storytelling, and story reading, and reading aloud may be part of a set of realistic objectives for the resource centre but this does not mean that the teacher-librarian alone must carry them out. Perhaps some program objectives would be better realized if sessions were held for classroom teachers on techniques and materials and if every teacher provided the service both in the classroom and in the resource centre.

From the aim, through the objectives, to the best methods of achievement, one must reach the question of priorities. How are priorities established for resource centre services? Indeed, are priorities established? Teacher-librarians as a group are sometimes guilty of perpetuating the myth that all teacher-librarians do the same things when in fact varying levels of support necessitate varying degrees of service. For example, a school of 350 students with a full-time teacher-librarian and aide should be providing a broader and deeper range of services than a teacher-librarian in the same size school who is part-time with no clerical help. Is this acknowledged, specified and articulated? Conversely, if the teacher-librarian is cut from full-time to part-time, or loses clerical assistance, is the effect known to everyone concerned? If there are no noticeable effects then perhaps there shouldn't have been that much staff to start with. Districts with strong support appear to have been successful with teachers, administrators and parents in making known, in terms specific to the instructional program, and the child's development, what the effects of cutbacks will be.

Teacher-librarians will always be called on to explain and defend their positions. This is a fact of life which applies to all nonclassroom positions, whether administrative, counselling, or learning assistance. The key here is that teacher-librarians are obviously not doing what could just as easily be done by a technician with a small budget or by the classroom teacher alone with thirty kids. And parents and administrators as well as teachers must understand this. And we have to tell them.

Hang Together or Hang Separately

Carol-Ann Haycock and Ken Haycock

When considering the role of the librarian in program advocacy, that is, explaining, defending, and recommending publicly the merit of library programs, it is too easy to feel that we are "out there" on a limb with no visible means of support. Too often we presume that no one is interested in speaking for libraries and librarians and that the first budget item to be cut will be library services. This strikes us as very peculiar.

Librarians are in the business of forming partnerships with colleagues and the community. We develop the foundation for advocacy for our programs but we rarely build on it, or in political parlance, we don't call in the chips or collect the IOUs.

We accept that librarians will communicate effectively with their administrations in oral and written form on a regular basis. We promote the role of the librarian in making presentations and leading workshops for parents and for colleagues. We accept as a given the development of teaching partnerships in schools and the close liaison between the children's and young adult librarian and related community groups. We work closely with related professional associations and publishers to develop efficient and effective systems for the selection and acquisition of materials and resource sharing among libraries. But we rarely draw on this strength.

How can this community knowledge of our programs and support for them be used? A recent example from the Vancouver, (British Columbia) School Board is worth sharing. In 1984, the government of British Columbia mandated a budget reduction of $16 million for Vancouver schools over three years. The board fought back through large public meetings, community support, lobbying, and even a court challenge—all to no avail. In spite of well-integrated, strongly supported library services, it was obvious that all areas of the system would be adversely affected and it was essential that the specifics of the program and its strengths be pointed out (again) to decision-makers. Strategy meetings were held and the process begun.

The format for response to proposed budget cuts was a series of public meetings. Since teacher-librarians, as members of a larger teachers' association, could not present a brief on their own, alternatives were sought. In the end, delegations were received and presentations made to the board. The professional teaching associations stressed the specifics of library development in Vancouver; the British Columbia Library Association stressed the importance of school libraries generally and the interrelatedness of all libraries; the Association of Book Publishers of British Columbia stressed the economic impact of cuts in materials budgets; parent consultative committees stressed the importance of full-time service for effective education for their children; community agencies (especially those concerned about specialized services, such as the "first language" collections), and retired teachers stressed the changes in teaching and learning made possible through effective library services. In addition, letters were received by the chairperson of the board from school staffs (stressing the negative impact of reduced library services on curricular programs in the school) and articles appeared in the local newspapers and the provincial teachers' association newsletter about the effect of proposed cuts.

When all was said and done, it became obvious that the district's school libraries were not only effective and warranted their present level of support (one full-time person at 300 enrollment and a protected budget of $30 per capita for materials—double the textbook allocation), but they were well-understood and supported in the schools and the community as well. Cuts were made—but not to the extent they could have been, particularly considering the elimination of complete programs in other areas and the layoff of more than 200 staff. The representations worked well and the knowledge provided will help to forestall additional cuts in the next two years.

The one major weakness, however, proved to be teacher-librarians themselves. A minority of teacher-librarians, through their local association and informal contacts, believed enough in the product to be effective spokespeople. Too many others, however, believed that either the situation was hopeless or that someone else would protect them or to prefer hand-wringing to concrete action. At all of these presentations and public meetings there were more supporters in the audience from outside the system than there were teacher-librarians. We are reminded of the saying "The meek may inherit the earth—but the news of it will never get out!"

When will we learn that it is no longer good enough to be even outstanding at our jobs in school while ignoring the need and potential for advocacy all around us?

You *Can* Make a Difference!

Ken Haycock

Rarely a day goes by when we are not confronted by yet another opinion poll about what we think, who we intend to vote for or what type of soap we buy. This fascination with the views of neighbors also extends to education with major polls nationwide and at the provincial/state levels, as well as those conducted by local school districts. Obviously, the view of the general public is not only considered, but perhaps even critical in decision-making and priority-setting.

School board chairpersons and superintendents have little option but to refer to polls and sometimes even delight in quoting those which support a particular viewpoint or reinforce what is being done or simply intended. The major studies conducted by Phi Delta Kappa (PDK) in the United States and the Canadian Education Association (CEA) in Canada, both in conjunction with the Gallup organization, tend to be the best-known, best-supported and most-quoted.

Teacher-librarians have much to learn about the value of these polls, and how to influence results and their subsequent use. Both the PDK and CEA polls include a wide range of questions addressing significant issues in public education. Respondents provide basic information on their place of residence, education level, sex, occupation, age, community size, income, mother tongue, children in school and previous contact with the schools, thus allowing for a detailed analysis of the views of various groups. Questions range from degree of confidence in schools compared to other public institutions to feelings about the strengths and weaknesses of different components of schooling, including perceptions of the quality of virtually every subject area and curricular emphasis. Of

course (!) library services are never mentioned so that concerned professionals might gauge the extent and location of support in the community at large, but then is it reasonable to expect teacher-librarians and their associations to request this simple addition?

In many parts of the world we are playing financial hardball to maintain school libraries. Cutbacks are forcing local school boards to sort out priorities rarely before being placed consciously on a fiscal ladder. Recent evidence shows, however, that teacher-librarians can made a difference to public attitudes and support for services, personnel and materials.

In the CEA poll, for example, respondents answered an open-ended question "in what areas are the schools in this community doing a particularly good job?" Interestingly, the second highest unsolicited response nationwide was "enrichment activities such as music events, tours, library services." In British Columbia, where an intensive community advocacy campaign for school libraries has been underway in several areas of the province, the results were almost double the national average. One can also conclude that the more adults are in schools, the better the support for school library services.

We need this documentation of the nature and extent of support in the community and we need it now. Lobby your associations to push for appropriate questions regarding school libraries on national and provincial/state polls, studies and surveys. And then make sure that your local community is aware of what you are doing. It really is the least you can do.

Where Do You Stand?

Ken Haycock

You have to wonder sometimes how often you can go on saying the same things year after year in the face of professional schizophrenia. I should warn you that this short piece started as a "notebook" entry, but soon became something more. It is really more the germ of about four articles, bordering on a diatribe, but perhaps you'll bear with me.

In today's mail came the California Media and Library Educators Association journal with an article by Herbert White on the "unity" of the library profession (11:2, Spring,

1988, pp.8-10) saying that "you will not be treated as equals if you are perceived 'only' as teachers who don't 'really' teach," and "librarians ... must first of all be librarians." At first we thought it was a historical piece, a reprint from 1954 for the archival types. Then we realized it was serious, and in a professional journal from a state that can't even get teacher-librarians in elementary schools! Why do we print this unsubstantiated, destructive material? Don't tell us for a different point of view! There are so many different points of view about school librarianship floating around universities that beginning teacher-librarians are being sold nothing more than a smorgasbord approach to professional training and socialization. When will we ever recognize a professional teaching role based on solid research? And communicate that clearly and forcefully with unity of mission?

On the other hand, of course, we have AASL touting the instructional consultant role in the new national guidelines (we'll run several reviews of this in the next issue). So, let's get this straight. We're confused about our professional role and status as teachers, and can't get acceptance as equal teaching partners, but we'll try and leapfrog the whole thing and make people realize we're actually better? That should engender support and good will! We're consultants now, instructional consultants. Even though we can't convince administrators to drop the library spare in order to develop a strong program. (We won't even get into that educational malpractice known as fixed scheduling!) Wow, what logic!

Well, at least we can always retreat into the reading program where we know we're loved and appreciated. Or can we? The same day we received the latest IRA title on exemplary reading programs. The characteristics of such programs included the following:

- shared assumptions that the school can make a difference, that all students can become literate, that teachers cooperate and work together, that the characteristics of effective schools are in place

- administrators and teachers who are committed to the change process with other personnel (particularly parents) involved

- staff development which includes all staff and is continuous

- curriculum implementation planned for an adequate time frame over a period of years.

So, where's the library? Where's the librarian? Can you believe it? They are not even mentioned. In planning for this publication is it possible that the editors never fell over a teacher-librarian? Or was the TL off in the library conducting literature appreciation classes to give the teacher a spare period? It would appear that we still have a long way to go. (We can only presume that our national associations draw these shortcomings to the attention of authors, publishers and related organizations which engage in perpetuating these problems.)

Teacher-librarians need to have a clear, defined role as professional teachers, specializing in the selection, management and effective use of informational and recreational resources. Their competencies need to include the ability to plan instructional programs with teaching colleagues that will develop in students the abilities, skills, and attitudes necessary for today's world. We need to speak with a unified voice about our role and communicate it effectively to school and district administrators and other teachers. Until then we will languish on the periphery of the educational program and wonder why we as librarians (much better than teachers!) aren't appreciated as an integral part of the teaching staff. It's about time that we all realized that teacher-librarianship is an integrated teaching partnership: recognized it, developed it and celebrated it.

A profession, however, is only as strong as its members. Where do you stand?

REFERENCES

Changing School Reading Programs; Principles and Case Studies edited by S. Jay Samuels and P. David Pearson. International Reading Association, 1988. 0-87207-790-X.

Information Power: Guidelines for School Library Media Programs, prepared by the American Association of School Librarians and Association for Educational Communications and Technology. American Library Association, 1988. 0-8389-3352-1.

Contributors

Larry Amey is associate professor at the School of Library and Information Studies at Dalhousie University in Halifax, Nova Scotia, where he teaches children's and young adult literature and media interests and school librarianship.

Bev Anderson was a teacher-librarian, coordinator of program resources, and elementary school principal with the Calgary (Alberta) Board of Education.

Julie Andreachhi is head of the resource center at Langstaff Secondary School in the York Region Board of Education, Aurora, Ontario.

Jim Bowman is a former school librarian, supervisor of library services, and superintendent of schools, and is currently director of the Government Division of the British Columbia Teachers' Federation.

The **British Columbia Library Association** is the provincial association of Librarians, other library workers, and friends of libraries; the BCLA does not include teacher-librarians and school resource centers in its primary mandate.

Gene Burdenuk was assistant professor of school librarianship at the University of Western Ontario Faculty of Education in London, and is currently director of the Educational Leadership Center at Western.

Pat Cavill has been the Director of the Marigold Library System in Strathmore, Alberta, since 1981; prior to that she spent 11 years in regional library development in Saskatchewan.

Linda Dunlop has been an English and world religions teacher and is currently head of the resource center at York Humber High School, Board of Education for the City of York, Toronto, Ontario.

Dean Fink is a superintendent of schools with the Halton Board of Education in Burlington, Ontario.

Shirley Fitzgibbons is assistant professor at the School of Library and Information Science at Indiana University in Bloomington.

Kathy Fritts is a former junior high school French teacher, ESL teacher in Samoa, apartment manager, and junior high school teacher-librarian. She now works as teacher-librarian at Putnam High School in Milwaukie, Oregon.

Thomas Hart is professor at the School of Library and Information Studies of Florida State University in Tallahassee, and chairperson of the legislation committee of the Florida Association for Media in Education (FAME).

Carol Hauser is a teacher-librarian at Colonel Irvine Junior High School in Calgary, Alberta.

Carol-Ann Haycock is president of the HRD (Human Resources Development) Group, a consulting and staff training group.

Ken Haycock is director of program services for the Vancouver (British Columbia) School Board and managing editor and publisher of *Emergency Librarian*.

Robin Inskip has a background in government and political science and is assistant professor at the University of Alberta Faculty of Library Science in Edmonton; she teaches marketing and chairs the Government Relations Committee of the Library Association of Alberta.

Ronald Jobe teaches courses in English education at the University of British Columbia in Vancouver; he is a former teacher-librarian and consultant with the Edmonton (Alberta) Public School Board.

Lorne MacRae is director of the media services group with the Calgary (Alberta) Board of Education.

Charles Parr is former state senator for District 20 in Fairbanks, Alaska.

Linda Rehlinger is a part-time teacher-librarian at Qualicum Beach Elementary School in school district #69 (Qualicum), British Columbia.

Mary Margaret Rogers is a professional library media specialist who was hired by the Florida Association for Media in Education (FAME) as part-time lobbyist in 1977, and has been association manager/lobbyist since 1980.

Sources

"Analyzing and Assessing Programs—Science/Resource Center Principles: For Every Action There Is a Reaction." Linda Dunlop and Julie Andreacchi. *Emergency Librarian* 15:5 (May-June, 1988), pp. 13-16.

"Building Consensus and Power in the Library Community: The Marketing of School Library Services by a Provincial Library Association." Robin Inskip. *Emergency Librarian* 11:4 (March-April, 1984), pp. 9-13.

"Commitments to Quality." [editorial]. Ken Haycock. *Emergency Librarian* 10:4 (March-April, 1983), p. 5.

"Hang Together or Hang Separately. [editorial]. Carol-Ann Haycock and Ken Haycock. *Emergency Librarian* 11:4 (March-April, 1984), p. 5.

"Hard Times ... Hard Choices." [editorial]. Ken Haycock. *Emergency Librarian* 9:5 (May-June 1982), p. 5.

"How to Get Your Legislator's Ear." Charles Parr. *Emergency Librarian* 15:5 (May-June, 1988), p. 27.

"How to Lobby by Letter, by Phone, in Person." Advisory Council on the Status of Women. *Emergency Librarian* 11:4 (March-April, 1984), pp. 15-16.

"The Importance of School Libraries/Resource Centers and Teacher-Librarians in British Columbia Schools." British Columbia Library Association. *Emergency Librarian* 10:5 (May-June, 1983), pp. 17-20.

"The Legislative Imperative for School Library Media Programs." Thomas Hart. *Emergency Librarian* 14:5 (May-June, 1987), pp. 19-21.

"Marketing Services for Young Adults in the School Library." Carol Hauser. *Emergency Librarian* 13:5 (May-June, 1986), pp. 21-23.

"On Jargon." [editorial]. Ken Haycock. *Emergency Librarian* 12:1 (September-October, 1984), p. 7.

"Plan and Target: Assess and Measure Public Relations Ideas That Work." Kathy Fritts. *Emergency Librarian* 14:5 (May-June, 1987), pp. 15-17.

"Power and the School Librarian—Starting Here, Starting Now." Jim Bowman. *Emergency Librarian* 9:1 (September-October, 1981), pp. 6-11.

"Professional Lobbyist and Volunteer Professionals: A Formidable Force for Advocacy." Mary Margaret Rogers. *Emergency Librarian* 14:5 (May-June, 1987), pp. 22-24.

"Program Advocacy: The Missing Element." Ken Haycock. *Emergency Librarian* 7:4-5 (March-June, 1980), pp. 3-4.

Pyramid Power: The Teacher-Librarian and Censorship." Larry Amey. *Emergency Librarian* 16:1 (September-October, 1988), pp. 15-20.

"Research on Library Services for Children and Young Adults: Implications for Practice." Shirley Fitzgibbons. *Emergency Librarian* 9:5 (May-June, 1982), pp. 6-17.

" 'Saying Farewell to Miss Prune Face'; or, Marketing School Library Services." Pat Cavill. *Emergency Librarian* 14:5 (May-June, 1987), pp. 9-13.

"School Libraries—A Rationale." Alberta Learning Resources Council. *Emergency Librarian* 11:4 (March-April, 1984), pp. 6-7.

"School Libraries—Definitely Worth Their Keep." Bev Anderson. *Emergency Librarian* 10:5 (May-June, 1983), pp. 6-11.

"Seven Steps to Developing Support from School Principals." Ken Haycock. *Emergency Librarian* 15:1 (September-October, 1987), p. 25.

"The Teacher-Librarian and Planned Change." Linda Rehlinger. *Emergency Librarian* 15:5 (May-June, 1988), pp. 9-12.

"Teacher-Librarian Collegiality: Strategies for Effective Influence." Ronald Jobe. *Emergency Librarian* 7:4-5 (March-June, 1980), pp. 5-8.

"Too Many Chickens ... Too Few Hogs." Lorne MacRae. *Emergency Librarian* 6:5-6 (May-August, 1979), pp. 8-9.

"The Trustee as School Library Advocate." [podium]. Ken Haycock. *Emergency Librarian* 14:5 (May-June, 1987), pp. 29-30.

"Twenty Ways to Invite School Board Members." Dean Fink. *Emergency Librarian* 15:1 (September-October, 1987), pp. 62-63.

"What Works: Research—The Implications for Professional Practice." *Emergency Librarian* 15:5 (May-June, 1988), p. 40; 15:4 (March-April, 1988), p. 38; 15:3 (January-February, 1988), p. 38; 15:2 (November-December, 1987), p. 38; 14:5 (May-June, 1987), p. 28; 14:4 (March-April, 1987), p. 34; 14:3 (January-February, 1987), p. 29.

"Where Do You Stand?" [podium]. Ken Haycock. *Emergency Librarian* 15:5 (May-June, 1988), p. 31.

"Who Speaks For Us? Power, Advocacy and the Teacher-Librarian." Gene Burdenuk. *Emergency Librarian* 11:4 (March-April, 1984), pp. 18-22.

"You Can Make a Difference!" [editorial]. Ken Haycock. *Emergency Librarian* 12:4 (March-April, 1985), p. 7.

Added Entry

Ken Haycock has also selected articles on the important theme of *The School Library Program in the Curriculum*. This title is a companion volume to *Program Advocacy: Power, Publicity and the Teacher-Librarian* and is also available from Libraries Unlimited. ISBN 0-87287-776-0.

The professional journal *Emergency Librarian* focuses on the role of the teacher-librarian in the school within the framework of cooperative program planning and teaching. Subscriptions are available for $45 or $40 prepaid from Dyad Services, Box C34069, Department 284, Seattle, Washington 98124-1069 [*in Canada*: P.O. Box 46258, Station G, Vancouver, British Columbia V6R 4G6.]

ABOUT THE EDITOR

Ken Haycock is director of program services for the Vancouver (British Columbia) School Board where he is responsible for developing and delivering curriculum and staff development programs and resources for more than 5,000 employees in 110 schools. The Vancouver School Board has policies mandating the role of the teacher-librarian within the context of cooperative program planning and teaching and flexibly scheduled resource centers. Ken is a past president of both the Canadian Library Association and the Canadian School Library Association. He has received the Queen Elizabeth Silver Jubilee Medal for contributions to Canadian society, the Margaret Scott Award of Merit for contributions to teacher-librarianship, the Grolier award for research in school librarianship and was recognized by Phi Delta Kappa as one of the 75 leading young educators in North America. He is publisher of the school library journal *Emergency Librarian*.

Index